Our thoughts are bees:
Writers Working with Schools

Mandy Coe and Jean Sprackland

First published in 2005
by Wordplay Press
61 Burnley Road, Ainsdale, Southport PR8 3LP UK
www.wordplaypress.com

ISBN 0-9549634-0-7

Supported by
Arts Council England
National Association for Literature Development
National Association of Writers in Education
Poetry Society
Writing Together

Cover design by Wordplay Press

ALSO BY MANDY COE
Pinning the Tail on the Donkey
The Weight of Cows

ALSO BY JEAN SPRACKLAND
Tattoos for Mothers Day
Hard Water

The Mind Poem

Thinking
is a beautiful use of a mind.
Our thoughts are bees
buzzing in the hive of our head.

The bees visit flowers
then return with ideas,
stories of butterflies,
dogs, cats, rabbits and grass.

Our blood runs like honey,
sticky with thoughts.

Year Five,
Kingsway Primary School, Wallasey

Contents

Foreword

There are some moments in a young life that can be truly life-enhancing, and deeply enabling and enriching. We all know this because we have been there as children. It can be the right word of encouragement and love at the right time from a parent. It can be a wonderful teacher conveying a passion for art, or literature or science. It could be a lark rising in the blue above a hillside, or a snatch of Mozart that touches the soul.

It is the business of schools to enrich and educate – without enrichment of the spirit, it is very difficult to educate at all, except in the most superficial sense of the word. To grow the seed, the soil must be fertile. We know that children who suffer from a poverty of experience, from negative relationships, from a lack of self-worth find it more difficult to thrive and find fulfilment as they grow up.

There are, of course, many ways to enrich the lives of children, to give them new insights into themselves and the world about them, and enable them to feel the power in their own creative wings. Inviting an author into school is just one of them, but given enthusiastic preparation and imaginative follow-up it can provide a child with just that much-needed spur to creativity, that boost in self-confidence which can enhance and enrich his life.

We know from recent research (we knew anyway) that 98% of children aged between two and three have a spark of genius in them, a light of unique creativity. Books can help, do help, to keep this spark alive. They give us knowledge, understanding and insight. They inspire us and trouble us. They keep us questioning. They tell us we are not alone in this world. They help us find our creative voices. But how best to bring books to children and children to books? Have parents read to them – it is the best start. Also teachers and librarians who love books themselves and have the time to read to the children - that way the children will catch that precious enthusiasm. Have libraries filled with light and colour, and peace, and have new books on the shelves. And have an author in the school.

But to make it work there has to be a sense of heightened awareness that this is special. Immerse the children in the writer's books so that they know that writer from the inside even before he or she walks in. Let it be a meeting of creative, enquiring minds – the reader and writer meeting face to face but through the words of the stories too. In such circumstances a writer in a school can indeed create moments that can be life-enhancing, life-changing even – can help a child become a reader for life, and maybe a writer too.

Michael Morpurgo (Children's Laureate, 2003 -2005)

Introduction

You begin by knowing nothing. It's the only thing you are sure of at the start. When taking part in an unfamiliar art-form, *I can't do this* is often the first thought. But the second thought – *I can't do this... yet* – should not be far behind. This leap of faith transforms our experience of culture. We become not only consumers, but also creators.

Supporting young people as they find their creative voice is an inspiring business. All of us – writers, teachers, and project co-ordinators – are thrilled by the sheer adventure of it. We listen to the plays, stories and poems young people write, and we are astonished. We value not only the art itself, but also the impact creative writing has on learning across the board. Writing creatively teaches us to think creatively, and the very act of *doing*, the act of *making*, changes us profoundly. Teachers understand this very well, and over the years have invited thousands of writers into their schools.

If you are a writer or teacher wanting to plan an author's visit for the first time, or a co-ordinator already running a range of activities involving writers and schools, this book is for you. It is organised in three sections, sequenced chronologically: **Before**, **During** and **After**. Each section contains detailed information on how to make your project a success.

There are as many approaches to the role of 'writers in school' as there are writers who do it, and our profession plays a dynamic role in education precisely because it harnesses such a diversity of expertise. Our research shows that the practice of visiting schools is particularly strong amongst poets; however, this is expanding to include writers in all disciplines. Writers-in-schools projects are happening every week across Britain and, although the traditional one-off author's visit is as popular as ever, new initiatives are more ambitious in scope and vision. The success of all of these ventures – one-offs and residencies – depends on teachers, writers, and project co-ordinators talking and listening to each other, receiving adequate training and understanding good practice.

Ours is a generous profession, and we were doubly glad of this as we aimed to reflect as wide a range of voices as possible, from England, Northern Ireland, Scotland and Wales. We consulted some of the most experienced professionals in this field. In addition, hundreds of questionnaires were distributed to co-ordinators, teachers, writers and pupils. We invited them to respond anonymously, to allow free expression of views and experiences, and many of these appear in the book.

We have both worked extensively as writers in schools, and when we were first approached to deliver training and consultancy on the subject, we searched for a book that covered the issues we encountered. Eventually we realised we would have to write it ourselves! As there was no central resource for this information, we faced a mind-boggling amount of research. We are deeply grateful to everyone who came forward to share practical advice, goodwill and their dreams for the future. Special thanks to our partners: The National Association for Literature Development, the National Association of Writers in Education, the Poetry Society and Writing Together.

Mandy Coe and Jean Sprackland

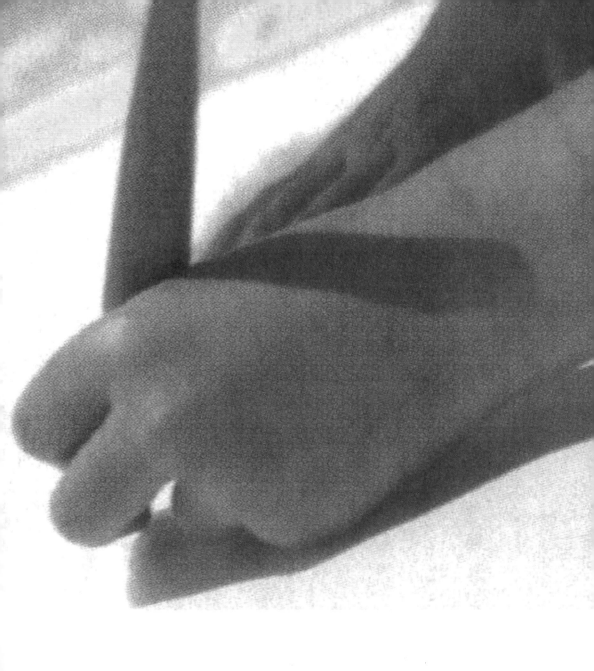

BEFORE

Making a start

"I'm not going to argue about this: I'm right. Children need art and music and literature; they need to go to art galleries and museums and theatres; they need to learn to play musical instruments and to act and to dance. They need these things so much that human rights legislation alone should ensure that they get them."
Philip Pullman (The Guardian)

Writers love spending time on creative work, and when we go into schools we find that young people love it too. The pleasure is contagious. In answer to the question 'What were the best things about the writer's visit?' a pupil replies: *"She gave us brilliant advice and she gave us lots of fun"*.

We are invited in by teachers who, in spite of the heavy demands of curriculum, timetabling and assessment, succeed in keeping creativity at the top of their agenda. They understand the principles of play and exploration that underpin the workshop. Liz Fincham, teacher and writer, says that *"English teachers are nothing if not subversive and so, when we are stymied by the system, we look for other ways to do what we believe in to foster creativity in our pupils. Without the chance to play about, experiment, jam, there can be nothing new, fresh, original, zany, inventive happening in classrooms"* (Writing in Education).

In this first part of the book we suggest ways to get started: finding the right writer, shaping and planning the project. But the very first step is the decision to give it a try. It's a powerful decision. As writer Rose Flint says: *"If a school cares enough about its students' creativity to bring in a professional artist of any kind, this sends a message to the pupils that this part of themselves is respected and valued"* (Writing Together).

Schools: finding a writer

So many great choices: fiction, non-fiction; playwrights, novelists, journalists, writer/illustrators, storytellers, comedy writers, poets, writer/performers. A number of organisations have extensive lists of writers who work in schools. So how do you go about selecting the right one for you?

The grapevine is a trusted method: a writer may come recommended by colleagues. Other writers are obvious choices because their work is included in the school library or curriculum; these can sometimes be contacted through their websites or via their publishers. Be warned though: there is a direct correlation between how well-known a writer is and the amount of advance notice needed for a booking. If you've planned well ahead, it's worth a try. But to broaden your choices, look at the organisations listed at the back of this book and start calling or surfing. There are hundreds of excellent writers out there.

The majority of requests for writers in schools are initiated by teachers. Most teachers say they want a writer who is:
- published;
- a good communicator and able to inspire;
- a positive role model, making a living out of writing and passionate about their work;
- flexible enough to make writing exciting and accessible to children of all abilities and a range of ages;
- genuinely interested in the work produced by students.

Writers work in different ways. Some prefer an 'author's talk' with questions and answers; others run workshops and encourage students to write themselves. Writers who incorporate humour and performance can entertain the whole school in the hall, while other writers prefer to read to a class. This diversity of approach reflects the infinite range of writing styles that exist in the world and the infinite ways in which young people can best become involved. As one teacher noted, it's important that writers *"like young people and are ready to remember what it felt like to be young and keen to write"*.

"It's vital for us to be prepared to look for 'relevance' or even 'irrelevance', in the widest possible array of talents. Not that we should begin to look on writers merely as passive collaborators who might be co-opted to shore up existing ambitions and intentions. We should look at them instead as people who can help to change the landscape. The fact of their difference in the classroom is crucial – however complementary it might be to teachers' own efforts."
Andrew Motion (Writing Together keynote address).

3

Finding a writer: a checklist for schools

Who?

- Poet, playwright, storyteller, novelist…?
- Do they have a publishing or performance history? (NB poets become established through performance/live literature as well as publication.)
- What experience do they have in schools? (Ask for references or word-of-mouth recommendation.)

What?

- Performance to whole school
- Readings to smaller groups
- Workshops
- Author's talk with questions

How?

- What age ranges do they prefer?
- Range of abilities
- Group sizes

Where?

- Booked directly or through a literature agency?
- Distance from the school
- Availability
- Fee and expenses

Can we…

- use the writer's visit to support a curriculum initiative?
- have a copy of the writer's bibliography, photo or cv to help prepare the school and students?
- accommodate the writer's needs for space and equipment?
- provide any special food requirements or overnight accommodation if needed?
- ask the writer to attend (paid) planning meeting/s (for a longer project) or contact them to chat about the day?
- offer the writer a lift, or give advice on local public transport links and taxis?

Writers: finding work in schools

Writers wanting to work in schools must be visible to them. Being published or winning literature prizes will help, but even this is not guaranteed to bring teachers to your door. The average person can name only a handful of contemporary writers, and half of those will be dead, so don't be offended if your name doesn't immediately come to a teacher's mind! Authors working regularly in schools have less of a problem, but everyone has to start somewhere.

Writers can take the initiative by contacting local schools or preparing a flyer. The 'scattergun' approach – mass mailing of letters or leaflets to schools – may get you a few bookings; however, schools receive a vast quantity of unsolicited mail every week. Your chances will be increased by ringing the school receptionist first and asking for the name of the Head of English or the Literacy Co-ordinator. Keep the flyer short: one side of A4 is ideal. Include:

- a lively, simple heading which states clearly what you are offering;
- a summary of your credentials as a writer (published/performed work);
- a brief description of your work (group sizes, age-groups etc);
- contact details;
- a short quote from a satisfied teacher, and contact numbers of two referees who know your work and have agreed to be contacted.

Be realistic. *"I am the Franz Kafka of the 21st century..."* puts people off, but a commendation from a co-worker or employer about a previous project will carry weight. When you finally get a booking, celebrate! If you impress teachers in one school they will tell colleagues elsewhere and things can snowball. Being able to earn a portion of your income through work in schools is rewarding and allows for flexibility, but remember, no matter how much time you spend seeking or delivering work in schools it is vital to go on writing, establishing yourself *as a writer*. This will always be at the centre of your education work, and it makes you increasingly attractive to schools.

Another route is to contact some of the many literature development organisations that exist across Britain. Each organisation works in its own way. Some initiate a limited number of projects a year, plan them in partnership and support the writer in situ. Others work more like agencies, responding to schools' enquiries by offering workshops delivered by writers on their books, and charging the school a fee for administrative support. We recommend that writers work for a variety of organisations, to experience different philosophies and working styles. Find out what exists regionally and nationally. Offer to meet co-ordinators and discuss project ideas, and ask them to keep your records on their books. Some organisations have web-based directories where you can register your details.

Negotiating the basics

However the school and the writer find each other, their first conversation is a chance to introduce themselves and sketch out the shape of the visit.

The first things to establish are: *Can the writer do it?* and *Does the writer want to do it?* He or she may want a few days to think before confirming the booking. If dates are not convenient it's worth asking whether they can be altered. When it's clear that the writer is willing and able, agree on a time to call and talk over plans.

In the case of a one-day visit, a phone call might be the only chance to establish how the day will go. Ideally it should be a conference between equal partners, but let's be honest: it doesn't always feel so straightforward. When you're on opposite ends of the phone line and saying hello for the first time, it's hard to know who should take the initiative, whose responsibility it is to bring things up. If one person sounds confident, knowledgeable and in control, the other may find it hard to ask questions or speak their mind. Crucial matters can be forgotten or swept aside.

The answer is to be prepared. Before you even pick up the phone, make a checklist so that nothing gets forgotten. Here are some basic points for teachers, writers and co-ordinators to discuss together:

What is the day all about? Is it a one-day visit or longer residency? (We look at the pros and cons in more detail in the next section.) Will there be workshops, a performance? Is it part of a Book Week, an Arts Festival, or is there a specific theme or curriculum focus? Generally speaking, the actual content of a workshop is best determined by writers, who are after all professionals, experts in their own field. With so many logistical matters to plan for don't let the substance and content of the visit go unmentioned! As David Smith of Mid Pennine Arts says, writers should *"make the most of their call to the school to discuss how they will work rather than just confirm the arrangements"*.

Group size and timetables *"The group has to be small enough for each pupil to play an active role... it is important not to mistake the visit for an exercise in Billy Graham style mass conversion, packing the assembly hall with the school's population. This might be OK for Ted Hughes or Kiri Te Kanawa, but it gives little contact between the child and the artist. Check with artists for the maximum size of the group they want to work with. Aim for that figure. It will mean disappointment for those who aren't included - but will also mean that those involved get the right attention."*
David Morley (Under the Rainbow: Writers & Artists in Schools)

Wishing to 'be fair to all the children', a school may request that the writer works with every class in the course of one day. In response to this, the writer and co-ordinator can make the point that 20-minute workshops (except with very young children) are not good value for money and don't allow much learning to take place. Small groups of 10 to 15 can be especially rewarding, but splitting a class has to be budgeted for as it means paying for a supply teacher. Remember to build in breaks for the writer to catch their breath and have a cup of tea. We look at suggested session times in *Timetabling*.

What age-group? It's important that writers are clear in their own minds about the age-groups they feel comfortable working with. On the phone, in the heat of the moment, it is tempting to agree to anything and everything: we all like to rise to a challenge! But a writer who is wonderful with older pupils can be utterly lost in a Reception class, while others are in their element in this environment but a bag of nerves with teenagers. As writers it is good for us to push our own boundaries, learn new skills and extend our range. But we also need to be honest with ourselves and the teachers about where our strengths lie.

Which pupils? The selection of pupils is usually the school's prerogative, although writers should be asked for their preferences. Wanting the writer to have a good experience and go away with a positive impression of the school, the teacher may suggest a 'top group' or choose pupils on the basis of good behaviour. Perhaps the writing day has been granted as a reward. However, there is an inclusion issue here, and many writers prefer to work with mixed ability groups.

Sometimes there is a specific focus; pieces of funding are given to schools by central government, ring-fenced for specific purposes to help meet the national priorities of the time, such as 'gifted and talented' pupils. If a project is paid for out of this money, its focus will be pre-set accordingly. In this case, the school and the writer can explore ways of fulfilling requirements while making sure that the project has an impact on *all* the pupils in the school.

Inclusion *"I worked nearly all morning in a class before discovering that one of the students was profoundly deaf. If I'd known in advance, the school and I could have made plans to include her."* As this writer's experience shows, inclusion needs to be mentioned at the onset. Writers don't want to be limited by preconceptions about the abilities or personal lives of individual pupils, but they will want to work with *all* the students in the room (these issues are covered in more depth in *Inclusion*).

Fees and payments Whether you state a standard fee or negotiate with each school, you need a 'ballpark' figure. Discussions about money can feel awkward, and knowing the going rate will give you confidence. Writers starting out may offer a cheaper rate, but all of us should be aware of the implications of under-cutting one another. At the time of going to press, both NAWE and the Poetry Society recommend a minimum of £250 per day for work with pupils, while Arts Council England recommends £300. This sum looks a lot less when you figure in that writers must set aside 28% of their earnings (over the personal allowance) to pay their tax and National Insurance and as self-employed people must provide for their own pension.

All these recommendations apply to a single day's work; longer residencies are often paid in one inclusive fee, which may represent a lower daily rate but is a welcome chunk of guaranteed income for the writer. Training trainers or INSET work with teachers commands higher fees, but should be offered only by writers with extensive experience in the classroom and an understanding of teachers' requirements.

Establish clearly at this stage that travel expenses are in addition and that accommodation is paid for by the school. Agree on the mechanics of payment and correct details for invoicing. Let the writer know when to expect payment. Time-consuming systems for processing payments can cause cashflow problems. Where possible, a cheque should be written and handed to the writer at the end of the day.

Materials and equipment What do we need, and who will provide it? As well as the basics of paper and pens the writer might use video, overhead projector or flip-chart. If photocopying is needed, the writer should send it to the school in advance. It's dangerous to walk into school at 9 am and expect to be able to get copying done for a 9.30 start.

Where? *Please* provide writers with maps and directions! Identify the nearest station and, if you cannot arrange to pick them up, give them the number of the taxi firm the school uses.

Hospitality If the teacher doesn't offer lunch, the writer should ask, mentioning any special dietary requirements. If it's a choice between a school dinner and taking sandwiches... take sandwiches.

Write down everything you've agreed, and put it in a letter. Congratulations! That one phone call will pay off on the day... and it's much easier next time around.

Day visit or residency?

"Multiple-visit writing projects are deeply satisfying because they enable a writer and a group of pupils to get to know one another and over time allow the writer to witness real development in their confidence and writing skills."
Neil Arksey

While many writers relish the possibilities residencies offer, it can be a struggle to commit to a longer amount of time, so the flexibility of day visits is also welcome. There are pros and cons to both, and each plays a valuable role.

Day visit

the pros

- It can act as a trial event. A longer visit can then be planned drawing on the experiences of students and staff.
- It's more affordable, and can celebrate a particular event, eg National Poetry Day.
- Writers are more likely to be available for a single day.
- The day can be made to feel special, a one-off where timetables are altered and a lunch provided for staff.
- In the rare instance of a writer not suiting the school's needs (or vice versa), the two will part amicably at 3.15!
- A well-planned day visit can be flexible and include a range of activities: performance, workshops, questions and answers.
- For writers, the 'routine' of day visits allows them to re-use tried and tested approaches, cutting down on preparation.
- It can be an exciting powerhouse event, a satisfyingly self-contained project, providing resources and ideas that continue to 'seed' writing activities for many days to come.

the cons

- If there is no follow-up, impact can be short-lived.
- The writer works with a smaller percentage of the students.
- No time to rehearse with the writer and build towards performance, exhibition or publication.
- Writers working mainly through day visits face unfamiliar journeys, timetables, colleagues and students.
- With no time to develop and edit student's work there can be a 'sameness' in the writing produced.

Residency

the pros

- The writer is able to build up a relationship with students and teachers.
- There is valuable time for INSET as well as the option of working with the wider school community.
- The writer is better able to take part in the embedding of the project into the school culture.
- Work with students follows a more natural pace, with time for drafting, editing and sharing writing processes, as well as developing new strands of work that reflect the interests of pupils.
- There is the option for work to reflect local issues and the possibility of exploring cross-curricular links.
- Individuals have the chance to participate and develop their writing in a wider range of ways.

the cons

- Increased funding and time commitment necessary from all partners.
- Residencies must be planned and booked well in advance.
- For writers, booked blocks of time can become an obstacle to committing to other work and writing time.
- If the writer is unsupported, the burden of responsibility and expectation can be stressful.
- If the project is not embedded and supported throughout the school the writer can feel isolated.
- For the writer, the development within the project means more preparation and follow-up time.

Thinking it through

Planning meetings should involve all partners. They offer a chance to thrash out hopes, expectations, roles and responsibilities. As we mention in *Evaluation*, this is a great time to generate the buzz of enthusiasm about new ideas that will drive the project to its conclusion.

Schedule the meeting well in advance of the start date, allowing time for everyone to put arrangements in place. If you are applying for funding, a lot of planning will get done in the course of filling in forms – a useful way of getting everyone 'singing from the same hymn-sheet'.

If plans have been finalised by the school and the project co-ordinator before the writer is appointed, an opportunity has been missed. The writer, an expert in this work, is an invaluable planning resource. Involving the writer early on will ensure that the project makes use of his or her strengths and interests, and will make for joined-up thinking.

"How do teachers find out how to support a writer in a school visit? It's difficult if it's your first time. I just asked the writer and she kindly shared resources and gave me lots of advice."
Teacher

Planning can be budgeted for
Finding time to plan can be problematic. Busy teachers have little time to sit down and talk things over thoroughly, never mind follow through or share information with colleagues. Meanwhile, writers are sometimes expected to attend planning meetings in their own time, free of charge. This is unacceptable. Planning is the key to a successful project. Funders know this, so include it in the budget so that people can be paid to do it properly.

Planning takes time
One of the factors which makes or breaks a project is the length of time available for planning and schools can drastically under-estimate this. Every year the Poetry Society receives calls from schools in the week leading up to National Poetry Day – sometimes the day before – requesting a poet. Even where a one-day visit is concerned, it's best to start the ball rolling at least one, preferably two terms in advance. Some writers are fully booked a year ahead. Many spend a great deal of time working away from home, and it may take a while to contact them.

Longer projects and residencies require longer planning horizons: we suggest a year wherever possible. This allows for proper consultation amongst staff, and for meetings and informal discussions where ideas have time to develop.

11

Preparing a proposal and budget for a funding application takes time. Find out when the funders' deadline falls and work back from that date.

Planning is an investment

One project co-ordinator urges writers to *"get to know as much as possible about the class and the specific aims of this visit, rather than delivering a standard multi-purpose workshop"*. Another feels that clear planning is never wasted: *"The plan can go out the window once the work starts, but it needs to be in place at the start. This is a chore for some writers, but you can't rely on instinct, inspiration and luck all the time"*.

One underlying problem is that the fees paid to writers do not always include an element for planning time, or time to develop specific workshop ideas and methods. Writers can take the lead here, pointing out that a residency should include some non-contact time, set aside for planning and preparation.

Planning pays dividends – it's an investment in your future as a writer in schools. You're building a repertoire of ideas and approaches which will stand you in good stead over the years and go on growing and evolving indefinitely. (For more information on training and professional development, see *Writers: keeping the balance*.)

Flexibility in the workshop

Schools or co-ordinators don't need to demand plans so detailed and definite that the writer feels trammelled. The point-by-point lesson plan sometimes required of teachers is not helpful when you're going to be working in an unknown environment with a group you've never met. Regard planning as a way of avoiding any nasty surprises, while leaving room for the nice ones. An experienced writer, used to 'thinking on his or her feet', will respond to the group's needs and enthusiasms and take advantage of serendipity: a news item which has captured the young people's interest, or an event in the life of one of their classmates. In an ideal situation, the writer will be well-prepared but confident and adaptable; while the teacher will trust the writer to make the right decisions and manage the session responsively.

"A huge electrical storm broke, with spectacular flashes of lightning and torrential rain battering the corrugated plastic roof. We were in the middle of some activity, but it was abandoned as we all rushed to the windows to watch. From then on, all the writing was full of extreme weather. It turned into one of the most successful sessions I can remember, with every single pupil fully engaged by the immediacy of the experience."
Writer

Planning a year

The school year has a shape and rhythm of its own, which helps in planning so that 'feast and famine' can be evened out. Seeing the year as a whole makes it easier for writers to achieve a balance between schools work and developing other aspects of their lives.

Schools benefit from long-term planning too. Rather than "Let's get a writer in this term", think of the shape of the year ahead, or even sketch in a three-year plan. This leads to more developmental projects with increased impact.

Prepare the class for the writer's visit

"I once had letters from a class of children who informed me that they had been told to write to me and that they hadn't read any of my poems but they felt sure that they were very good."
Brian Moses (Inviting a poet into your school)

If possible, involve students in planning the project. They can help make decisions on group sizes, who is to participate, what outcomes they would like, and what genre of writing they would like to explore. Preparation should include spending time with the pupils revisiting work they have done in this chosen genre, reminding them of terms and techniques they may have touched on previously. They can also be set a research assignment to find out about the writer through texts and the internet.

Allow yourself time to obtain the author's books and introduce them to your students. As Sasha Hoare, Education Officer at the Royal Festival Hall, puts it: *"Build up to the visit in advance by reading the writer's work in class, talking about them and generally preparing the children so that it doesn't feel so 'parachuted in'".* When asked what three things would make her work in schools more rewarding, Jackie Kay said: *"Small workshop groups; teacher participation; and students reading at least one poem of mine before I get there"* (www.poetryclass.net).

If the writer doesn't bring up the subject of books in the initial phone call or planning meeting, the teacher should make a point of asking. The writer may be able to supply books or put the teacher in touch with the publisher. A poet's work may be featured in anthologies which are already on the school bookshelves or could be ordered (start this process well in advance). In some cases, not all the writer's published work will be suitable for the age-group in question, and in others the work will be for performance or broadcast rather than publication on the page. Ask the writer for help in sourcing the right material.

Teacher as reader

It's an added delight for the writer when a hard-pressed teacher has made time to do a little reading; it means the teacher will have learnt something about the writer's style, themes and preoccupations, which gives the project a head start. Too often, teachers are so intently focused on the outcomes they hope for in the classroom that they leapfrog clean over the writing itself. The whole day – the whole project – can go by without the writer's own work being mentioned once. This is demoralising for the writer and a wasted opportunity for the school. As one writer says, *"the worst thing is when you're walking down the corridor and the teacher says* What's *your name?".*

Finding the money

Writing Together suggests the following ways of raising the money within school:

- school budget – your headteacher might consider funding a writer's visit directly;

- Standards Fund – if the visit can be combined with some opportunity for teachers' professional development (through participation or observation) it is perfectly legitimate to use this budget;

- School Fund or Parent Teachers Association – make a case for the visit and see if it can be paid for from these sources of extra funding;

- fundraising events which can also help to build interest in creative writing and reading – like selling a book of poems by pupils, organising a reading for parents, or a sponsored write-in.

If you're thinking of applying for funding from an external source, the following pages will help: Abigail Campbell of Arts Council England offers some dos and don'ts to improve your chances of success.

Funding applications: golden rules

Know your funder
The easiest way to interest a funder in your proposal is to write it well and with focus. Spend time researching funding opportunities and make sure you apply to the most relevant source. Look on the application as an opportunity to explain to a funder how your project will help them meet their aims.

Once is rarely enough
Avoid the one-off and the in-out. Think about maximising the effects of each activity and of sustaining the benefits. This isn't necessarily about the numbers of people taking part. It's about making sure that you can embed whatever experience you are offering in the life of the school and its wider community.

Strength in numbers
Many public funders will not fund individual schools for individual projects. Consider the benefits of developing a consortium of local schools, or of working with a local arts organisation, library or community group. This way there's more support for you and a wider audience for the activity.

Who, me?
Spell out the benefits of your project to participants and audiences. But also take a step back and think about what you are going to get out of this experience. Consider your own professional development needs and interests and include them in an application, costing them where appropriate.

State the obvious
Never assume that your prospective funder knows what's going on inside your head. Too often applicants leave out the filling in the sandwich and don't describe what will actually happen and how. Imagine you are in the audience at your event: How will you feel? What will you be doing? What is so important about it? Describe how you will manage the activity: Who will do what, and when? Answering these questions well will reassure your funder that the project is valuable and that it stands a realistic chance of success.

Do the maths
Spend plenty of time on your budget. Break it down as far as you can. Avoid guesswork by getting quotes in advance. And make sure the budget balances.

Start early and finish late
It takes time to apply for public funding. Funders are accountable and need to observe due care in their application procedures. So, be prepared to put in time

to research, consult and plan, and also to review and document your activity. A meaningful evaluation will not only help you attract future funding, it will help you plan for your next project.

Information sheets on a number of these areas (eg How to pay artists, and Self-evaluation) are available to download from www.artscouncil.org.uk.

Where to apply?
There are too many sources to list here, but you can now find clear and comprehensive information on funders for schools projects, all in one place: go to www.readingconnects.org.uk and click on **Funding**.

Evaluation

Good evaluation is the dinner-date we dream of: it's interested in what we do, our aims, hopes and successes. So what puts us off? The very word 'evaluation' makes many of us yawn and shift in our chairs, picturing a flip-chart covered in acronyms like SARNIES and STUMPS. This is where red *and* blue marker pens are needed.

There isn't space here to describe every method of evaluation, but we are aware that people reading this might be first-time or reluctant evaluators, and we want to argue that proper evaluation can be a positive experience rather than an obligatory chore. A human-friendly, well-designed evaluation form should make you close your eyes and really remember. It will nudge you to recall how well you did and *what you might do next time to make it even better.*

Evaluation for group projects
"Rigorous evaluation enables all of us to accumulate a collective body of evidence which contributes to the 'collective practice wisdom of the sector', building a record of our 'history and achievement'."
(Evaluating Community Arts and Community Well Being)

It all starts with the **aims**. You might want to give your secondary pupils a deeper understanding of how a play gets written, or a newspaper is put together. You might want to build links with your local library by writing poetry for display there. It seems simple: you have a project. You plan it, put it into action, and afterwards you discuss whether it worked or not. So doesn't evaluation come at the end? Maybe this would do for the simplest activity, like getting up out of a chair; but for anything more complex, begin by asking one simple question: *has your project been done before?*

Enormous amounts of time and energy can be saved by talking to someone who's already undertaken a project similar to yours. If asked, funders or project partners will put you in touch with people who will be only too happy to share their experiences and evaluation. Two questions: *What really worked?* and *If you did it again, what would you do to make it better?*

We might be individualistic in the arts, but reinventing the wheel over and over is a task that drains excellence and energy from our work. Funders (whose role is to provide advice as well as money) will be so impressed you are doing evaluation at the planning stage that they will give you money to do it. Yes, you can budget for it! Costs can include:

- paid planning meetings for writers and teachers;
- employing an independent evaluator;
- gathering evidence, including photos, quotes, newspaper coverage;
- designing and printing fun, feed-back forms for participants.

Discussing what you want to achieve is an ideal time for blue-sky thinking – a wonderful, visionary stage of the project. Energy and enthusiasm feed the buzz that makes a project special. What would you like to happen? Have a few fantastic aims, crossed-fingers ones and plenty of achievable ones too because whether or not you achieve your aims will help you measure your success.

Don't forget that evaluation is not just about planning at the start and noting achievements at the end. Mid-project meetings allow a venture to alter (or get back on) course, as well as providing opportunities for co-ordinators to collect evidence and address unexpected issues.

Back to that chair we mentioned earlier. *Experience more physical activity* might be an appropriate aim. But if it's a tired teacher or writer sitting there, with a remote control and a bottle of wine, this aim needs to be broken down into a clear set of achievable **objectives**... starting with *Fetch bottle opener.*

Once you have agreed on your objectives, you need to consider how you will measure whether or not you have reached them. Your measures of success can involve arts learning, personal and social development and other benefits. Some **measures of success** might be:
- half the pupils in year 5 become regular users of the public library;
- ten pupils from year 9 devise and write a play;
- school newspapers are created and distributed by year 8;
- at least 80% of pupils experience teamwork;
- participating pupils work with a professional writer.

So far we have identified **aims** (*the dream);* **objectives** (*specific tasks to achieve the dream);* and **measurable successes**. To measure these successes you need to gather **evidence**, and you should collect it right from the beginning. It's *the proof you need, to show what you've achieved*: facts and figures (quantitative evidence); and opinions and feelings (qualitative evidence). The good news is that you will amass some of it anyway through documentation: notes, photos, letters and contracts. But other evidence needs a little more effort to collect.

One way students can take part in evaluation is by designing evaluation forms. They can include pictures, smiley faces or star ratings (see *Evaluation Resources* and *Websites* and for more on this). Discovering the attitudes of the participants before the activity begins gives you a baseline by which you can

18

measure changes. For instance, in one writer's visit to a school on Merseyside, the children were asked, at the start, to write down what they felt about writing a poem:

- *"I sometimes don't know where to start."*
- *"I don't know how to rhyme because the words don't fit."*
- *"I worry that I'll have nothing to write."*

Afterwards they were asked the same question again:

- *"I learned to redraft so it can rhyme if I want."*
- *"I am more confident in getting ideas."*
- *"We can make up stories about anything we want."*

Here are some other ways of collecting evidence:

- diaries, meeting notes;
- videos and photos, recordings*;
- finished and draft work;
- contracts, programmes, publications;
- press cuttings and audience attendance records;
- questionnaires and/or comments and quotes.

Some of the evidence will measure your successes; other evidence will be useful for **documentation**. Make sure all methods of collecting evidence are user-friendly and not intrusive within the sessions; and that their design and delivery takes into account equal opportunities issues.

A successful project will result in a number of **outcomes**. Here are a few common to writer-in-schools projects:

- the work! (the art produced and the process are both valid outcomes);
- increased understanding of issues dealt with in the project;
- an observable increase in skills (writing, researching, editing etc);
- stronger links between school and the wider community.

You may also find **longer-term outcomes**, such as:

- raised expectations and standards;
- partners more confident in investing in future projects/training;
- positive influence on leisure or career choices.

During the evaluation of a primary school project in Liverpool, pupils were asked 'Do you think you learnt some new skills to help you with future work?'. One pupil replied: *"My mum has been telling me that I could be a poet because I've got a pad full of them so I would like to be a poet and show what I can do and not be ashamed"*.

* publishing or broadcasting young peoples' names or photos raises issues of safety and child protection. For guidance see *Good Practice*

Involve the children and young people in the evaluation from the start. It is an important chance for them to learn and be empowered. Evaluation lets everyone see what's been achieved. It lets you discover not only the immediate and long-term **benefits**, but positive changes you didn't even plan for (**unexpected outcomes**). For example, a project may lead to permanent changes in the school or community; or to requests for further training. Even more reasons to celebrate!

"What did I personally get out of the writer's visit? A more creative side of me."
Pupil

Self-evaluation for writers

A working knowledge of evaluation will aid you in applications for grants, bursaries and jobs. But evaluation is also an invaluable way of learning. It provides a structure for analysing your activities and, through reflection, encourages you to assess your existing methods and consider how you can develop them. The following questions are for freelancers working with Grosvenor Museum in Chester. They encourage honesty, but also feel supportive and non-judgemental:

Self-evaluation: sample questions

- Describe the general feel of the group/visit.
- How do you think the group reacted to the activity?
- How fully did the group participate in the activity?
- Was there anything that particularly stood out about the activity or the group's reaction to it?
- Is there anything about today's activity that you would now change?
- How do you think the group responded to you as a facilitator?
- As a facilitator are there any areas you need to develop?
- What did you get out of this workshop?

In a wider sense, self evaluation helps us avoid the trap of short-term thinking. Writers responding to one job request after another often have little time to plan ahead, and this reactive rather than proactive way of working can be countered through self-evaluation. Evaluation reminds us of what we have achieved, while helping us with longer-term career aims by identifying practical steps we can take to achieve them.

Evaluation resources:

Partnerships for learning: a guide to evaluating arts education projects
Felicity Woolf (Arts Council England, 2004)
Useful to anyone who organises participatory arts projects specifically focusing on education. The revised edition can be downloaded from www.artscouncil.org.uk

Arts Council Evaluation Toolkit
an interactive online resource available at www.evaluationforall.org.uk

Monitoring and evaluating your arts event: Why bother?
(Voluntary Arts Network, 2003)
This guide is straightforward and suggests less conventional methods for gathering information from young people. Sample questionnaires are included.
www.vaw.org.uk (click **VAW publications**, then **Other publications**).

Built-in, not bolt-on: engaging young people in evaluation
Swords, M (New Opportunities Fund, 2002)
This report discusses practical ways of involving young people in consultation and evaluation. The report is listed as *Engaging Young People Report* on www.nof.org.uk (follow links to **Evaluation/Research**, then **E&R publications**).

Why writers in schools?

Inspiration, excitement, enjoyment, love of words: when a school and a writer get together, they make a kind of magic. Young people become real writers, taking possession of language and learning to make themselves heard. Sue Hackman, National Director of the KS3 Strategy says: *"Any teacher in any class may be nurturing the great novelists, poets or playwrights of tomorrow. What better apprenticeship can there be than watching successful writers working with their raw materials?"*. But this is only half the story. Only a few young people will write for a living, but every single one deserves the chance to become articulate, confident, skilled with words, an enthusiastic reader.

In *Writers: Keeping the Balance* we look in detail at why writers choose to work in schools. As far as schools are concerned, planning and organising a writer's visit or residency takes time, energy and money; but as teachers who have run successful projects in their schools will tell you, it's worth it! Teachers, writers and co-ordinators know that the project offers something special, something not available from the school's internal resources.

What is that something? Can it be identified, described or examined? The work of writers in schools has evolved organically over the past 40 years or so, having its roots in the community arts movement. Much of it is underpinned by a faith in the power of art to transform individuals and societies. Here we look at some of the ideas that motivate us.

CREATIVITY

"Creativity is at the heart of being human: a defining feature of our intelligence and sensibility. Creativity drives human culture on every front. Developing creative abilities is a basic function of education: and the need is becoming more urgent."
Sir Ken Robinson (Times Educational Supplement)

Teachers know that projects with writers can give a huge boost to the creative life of the school. In recent years they have sometimes felt they were swimming against the tide, but now, after many years of 'back to basics' the policy pendulum has begun to swing back again.

All Our Futures This landmark report to Government by the National Advisory Committee on Creative and Cultural Education in 1999 made the case for a greater emphasis on creativity – not as a distraction from core concerns with literacy and numeracy, but as *"equally relevant to the needs of this and future generations"*. The National Campaign for the Arts continues to lobby and campaign on the strength of the report.

Excellence and Enjoyment In May 2003, the Department for Education and Skills (DfES) published this Strategy document for primary schools in England. It advocates greater creativity, placing it at the centre of teaching and learning. The word 'creativity' here does not refer exclusively to artistic activity, but applies across the board to exciting, engaging experiences in the classroom.

Expecting the unexpected This was followed in August the same year by an HMI publication, subtitled *Developing creativity in primary and secondary schools*. This was the report on a survey to identify good practice in the promotion of creativity in schools in England. Amongst other things, this document praised schools which *"valued external expertise and perspectives"*, including those of artists and writers. It highlighted cases which had helped teachers think afresh about how they teach and how pupils learn: *"Crucial in this respect has been the role of artists, whose working methods have helped teachers to review familiar pedagogical practices and to try new approaches."*

A number of current initiatives have played their part in boosting the currency of 'creativity', including:

- **Artsmark** *"A recognition and reward scheme for schools dedicated to the arts"* (though its core definition of the arts does not include literature or creative writing). The scheme operates in England only.
- **Creative Partnerships** Launched in 2002, the DCMS/Arts Council England flagship programme in the cultural education field. It focuses on neighbourhood renewal areas; the idea is to give school children aged 5-18 and their teachers the opportunity to explore their creativity by working on sustained projects with creative organisations and individuals (some but not all of them artists).
- **Excellence in Cities** A targeted programme of support for schools in deprived areas of England. EiC provides resources and strategies focused on teaching and learning, behaviour and attendance, and leadership. The programme is delivered locally by schools working in partnership with their local education authority. It is not an arts-specific programme, but has funded and enabled many creative projects.
- **Specialist Arts Colleges** There are currently 304 secondary schools, specialising in the media, performing, or visual arts, plus a further 12 combining the arts with another specialism.

The result of all this is that schools are now being positively encouraged to 'be creative'. This is an exhortation some teachers find a bit galling, especially in the context of so much in the way of targets, testing and league tables. Finding funds for projects remains a challenge for some schools.

LITERACY

"Writers can enable young people to express and value their own ideas and opinions, a prerequisite for effective communication. An exact command of language enhances work in all subjects and is at the heart of successful relationships, social and intellectual."
David Morley (Under the Rainbow: Writers and Artists in Schools)

At the time of going to press, an entitlement is being drafted which would guarantee a range of creative reading and writing opportunities throughout school life, including work with a writer. This is part of English 21, a major research exercise on the future of English in schools.

Literacy has always been central in schools, but in recent years the word itself has acquired a new – and political – currency. The wave of panic over standards of reading and writing among school leavers, and the introduction of the National Literacy Strategy in primary schools in 1998, affected the work of writers in schools in dramatic and complex ways, at least in England (schools in Northern Ireland, Scotland and Wales are not required to adopt the Strategy; their devolved governments have given them 'local discretion' to pick and choose what they see as its best features).

Initially, many primary schools were implementing the Strategy in rather rigid ways which left little room for anything 'different' like work with a writer. Even in schools which continued to make space, teachers would express surprise at the relevance of the writer's work to the objectives in the Framework; one writer relates that at the end of his session the teacher said in tones of amazement: "You've just done a Literacy Hour!". The writer had neither studied the Framework nor set out to comply with it; a good workshop with a writer will *naturally* hit many of the targets and objectives teachers are required to achieve. There is both anecdotal and hard evidence indicating that extended work with a writer can raise standards; there are examples of dramatic improvements in SATs results (achievement to Level 4 up from 48% to 79% in one case).

Once schools adjusted to the Literacy Strategy, absorbed it and made it their own, fortunes turned: far from making writers less welcome in schools it became one of the justifications for inviting them in. Poets were particularly in demand; the Framework features poetry in every term of every primary school year, and some teachers, living with the legacy of poor or non-existent poetry teaching in their own schooldays, felt uncertain about their competence in this area. A visit by a poet was seen as a way of supporting and resourcing teachers, as well as a good experience for pupils.

Writing across the curriculum The focus has now shifted: in 2003 the Literacy and Numeracy Strategies were taken under the umbrella of the Primary National Strategy and the Key Stage 3 National Strategy. These cover teaching across the entire curriculum. It's no longer unusual for writers to receive requests to lead writing workshops within History, Maths or Science lessons. Many skills and methods are transferable between all kinds of writing, whether it's a ghost story, a sonnet or the write-up of a Chemistry experiment. Drafting, for example, is often cited by teachers as an area where they welcome input from practising writers. The one-day visit may be limited to exercises for 'getting started', but longer projects offer opportunities to explore the redrafting that is such a big part of the creative process. Anthony Wilson, reflecting on a residency with Year 8 pupils, speaks of the importance of moving on beyond that first stage and offering pupils real tools for the job, *"to the point of bringing in photocopied drafts of my own poems, to show the halting and intimate moments of how some poems get written... where one starts to order and to shape the marvellous information the brain releases when it is given the right conditions"* (Writing in Education).

How far to 'go along' with the structures and policies that shape school education is an issue for every writer to grapple with. A few writers refuse to have their work included on any curriculum list or exam syllabus. Others have formed a group, Authors Against the SATs, which campaigns for the abolition of Standard Assessment Tests, saying: *"We think that children's understanding, empathy, imagination and creativity are developed best by reading whole books, not by doing comprehension exercises on short excerpts and not from ticking boxes or giving one word answers. It is our view that reading for pleasure is being squeezed by the relentless pressure of testing and we are particularly concerned that the SATs and the preparation for them are creating an atmosphere of anxiety around the reading of literature."*

WRITER AS ROLE MODEL
"We acknowledge all the teachers who know that a hero can fire up imaginations, and bring all sorts of heroes into their classrooms."
New Zealand Book Council

We live in a climate where many young people – especially young men – feel excluded from the world of books. Teachers and project co-ordinators look to other adults to model different attitudes, lifestyles or values. Fiction for 'reluctant readers' is almost a genre in itself, and some writers respond so effectively to this challenge that they and their books are in constant demand by schools; teachers watch with delight as their pupils actually *enjoy* reading.

The need for specific role models is also cited in schools where a large proportion of the pupils are from minority ethnic communities; black students may for example have encountered images only of white writers. It is felt that a carefully chosen writer can offer a positive image which may challenge young people's expectations and broaden their horizons.

"When asked what they thought a poet would look like, all the kids in Meadows School said they thought I would wear a suit; one thought I would wear a cravat and talk posh. 'But he's not like that,' said another – 'he's got a face and everything!'"
Andy Croft
(www.poetryclass.net)

CREATING CONFIDENCE
"If you're not keen on school and not very happy, working with someone like a friend can encourage you to come to school."
Pupil (Artists Working in Partnership with Schools)

Teachers note improvements in confidence and self-esteem among pupils who have worked with a writer. The invitation to write can offer a chance of self-expression to a young person who has previously felt 'voiceless'. It can be an opportunity for young people to 'speak out' on specific issues, such as bullying or racism – in fact, entire writing projects can be built around issues that fit in with a wider agenda within school, or as a collaboration between different curriculum areas such as English and Citizenship. There is growing interest in the importance of 'emotional literacy'; in the words of the writer Graham Mort, *"young people's lives are not easy and many of them are struggling to understand their own responses to what happens to them. The emotional exploration - and discipline - of poetry can bring those feelings within reach, project them into the public domain, and shape them in a positive way"* (www.poetryclass.net).

A writing project brings novelty and variety into school life – things which can help reinvigorate bored and disaffected young people. When asked "What were the best things about the writer's visit?" one pupil replied: *"Missing lessons"*! A new adult into the classroom – one who reinforces the school's view that reading and writing are important, but occupies a less formal role and speaks from different life experience, can affect young people deeply. One pupil wrote to a visiting writer: *"All the time you have been coming, every week you have made me feel like a different person"*.

TEACHER'S LEARNING
A writer's visit is not only for the pupils; it can also be a powerful experience for teachers. This subject is explored in more depth in *Roles in the Classroom*.

Potential benefits include the chance to see another style of delivery, another way of working with language; an exchange of teaching ideas; the chance to observe pupils interacting with another adult; and a greater understanding of the skills and processes involved in writing. Taking part in a workshop is a crucial experience which can influence teaching for years to come. As one teacher so clearly puts it: *"Imagine a music teacher who will not play an instrument or an arts teacher who refuses to draw!"*.

SUPPORTING THE CURRICULUM
Students studying for GCSE and A'Levels, or Standard Grades and Highers/Advanced Highers, can benefit from the input of a professional writer on the texts or the issues they face in their courses. The carefully chosen writer will help students 'get inside' a text by looking at it *as writers*, whether it's a monologue poem, reportage or classic fiction. The wealth of choices writers make – about character, setting, tense, vocabulary, sentence structure, punctuation – come alive when seen from an insider's point of view.

ENJOYMENT AND CELEBRATION
The sheer delight of a writer's visit can be an end in itself, either as a one-off or as part of a more ambitious project such as an arts festival. These often take place towards the end of the summer term, when exams are over and the school wants to offer pupils a different pace and style of learning.

In the maelstrom of activity surrounding a festival, it's important that the school remains clear about the contribution a writer can make, and chooses the right writer for the job. Writers can sometimes feel under pressure to put on an all-singing, all-dancing show. While there may be a few who can do that without breaking sweat, for others it's incompatible with their personality or style of work.

Arts festivals are happy and celebratory occasions, offering exciting opportunities for the writer to collaborate with artists in other disciplines and to work with young people in a more relaxed way.

Other literary, religious or cultural events can be celebrated by a project with a writer: National Storytelling Week, World Book Day, International Mother Language Day, National Science Week, International Literacy Day, International Women's Day, Book Week and National Poetry Day, to name but a few! At the back of the book we recommend websites that provide calendar listings.

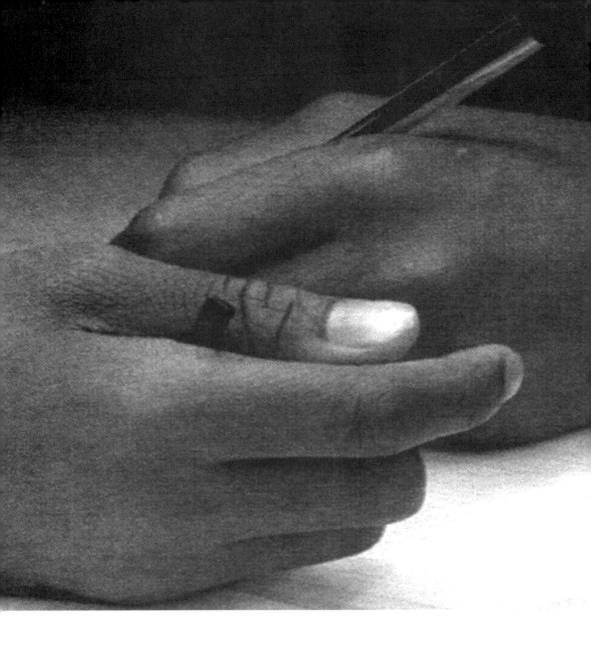

DURING

Live Literature

"Telling stories is as basic to human beings as eating. More so, in fact, for while food makes us live, stories are what makes our lives worth living."
R Kearney (On Stories)

Robert Frost once said: *"Words exist in the mouth not in books"*. Live literature is fundamental to what writers can do in schools, and there are development organisations which can offer advice. The Verbal Arts Centre in Northern Ireland provides a wealth of support for activities in schools; the Scottish Storytelling Centre has a searchable database of professional storytellers; Apples & Snakes runs a Poets in Education Scheme, promoting poetry that is "accessible to the widest possible range of people".

In the following pages, three writers explore aspects of live literature in schools: performance poetry, scriptwriting and storytelling.

Poetry and performance

Levi Tafari

When exploring poetry and performance with students in school, I usually start from a point of cultural and self awareness, as poetry is an internal/spiritual experience that is inspired by the external environment. I introduce myself, and talk about why I started writing, what inspires me to write. After a short performance, we proceed to explore the link between language and our day-to-day activities, and how poetry is created out of this experience.

We look at how similes, metaphors, alliteration and personification are used generously in our everyday speech, and can effectively be turned into poetry by applying style, form and rhythm/metre. We also discuss 'to rhyme or not to rhyme'. We look at repetition, the mood and the tone of a poem and how to mind-map a poem for ideas through word selection.

I find that the playing of word and rhythm games adds another dimension to the session, and helps the students build confidence and work together. The students should now be ready for the challenge of writing a poem, either on their own, in pairs or in small groups. Students who may lack confidence in an academic sense find that through the creative process they rise to the challenge of expressing themselves. They are pleasantly surprised to find that they too can write a poem. You can see the students' confidence grow as they open up. It's a beautiful, uplifting sight.

The space I work in makes a difference to the atmosphere, whether it is a classroom, drama studio, library or a school hall. I also make sure the school can provide the resources I need, like an overhead projector or a sound system with recording facilities - it's a good idea to record performed poems.

I really enjoy working at a school for a few days. It allows me to build a relationship with the school and its students. Working with fewer groups gives me time to develop work that has quality and depth and can be performed. I was fortunate to work on a Poetry Carnival in Cheshire a few years ago. I worked with the English department on writing, the Art department on creating masks and costumes, and the Music department, adding percussive rhythms. The theme allowed us to include a multicultural element to the work. It was an exhilarating experience working across the curriculum, with a multimedia, multicultural emphasis. The results were remarkable.

Levi Tafari has three collections of poetry, and his work has been included in many anthologies. He visits schools, colleges, universities and prisons in the hope of inspiring the new generation of performance poets. He has been poet in residence with The Royal Liverpool Philharmonic Orchestra and has toured with the British Council in the Czech Republic, Jordan, Portugal, Germany and Singapore.

Dramatic writing
Tracy Aston

What I love about a play is the immediacy of the experience. I've often struggled to get through novels which have a lot of descriptive passages, however beautifully written, and have found myself thinking, 'Get on with it!' I get impatient when it comes to story. I also like the challenge of having to establish characters, include any necessary information and set the story in motion all at the same time. And then there's the joy when a character suddenly jumps off the page. It's like discovering the solution to a puzzle.

When I work with younger children, I usually begin with character, using items of clothing and objects as starting points. Through simple questioning involving the whole class, characters quickly begin to take shape. Initially, all ideas are taken on board, there are no wrong answers at this stage, which encourages children to contribute. They are then free to cherry-pick the ideas that interest them most. Children work individually or in smaller groups to develop additional characters, and from these, storylines. The children improvise around their ideas to see what works before beginning to commit their script to paper. Starting each session with drama games helps to focus the group, encourage them to work collaboratively and use their imaginations.

With Year 9 and above, photographs of people, newspaper cuttings or a theme are all interesting ways to start. Or I use a simple exercise where the class draws up a love and hate list – anything from *chocolate* and *kindness* to *injustice* and *my brother*. I'm asking the students to consider what they feel most strongly about, not only ensuring their interest but also setting the basis for conflict, which is essential for both drama and comedy.

I believe that dialogue is something that can't be taught. It's about listening – or rather hearing – the rhythms and patterns of speech, and being able to reproduce them. Improvisation allows the children to experiment until they hear what sounds right. Hot-seating can also be used to develop a character collaboratively.

Some projects involve a whole class in the writing of one play. I enjoy longer projects like these; they allow time to develop work in more depth and bring it to life in performance.

Tracy Aston's work includes six plays for BBC Radio 4; *Playing God* and *The Frog Prince* at Unity Theatre Liverpool; *A Winning Combination* for Altrincham High School; *All Work, No Play* for Dorchester Youth Theatre; and *The Fearsome Seed* for Kilpeck Youth Theatre.

Storytelling is universal
Sandra Agard

Everybody tells each other stories. They don't have to feature Cinderella, a ghostly happening or Anansi the Spiderman; it could be what you did over the weekend, or what programmes you watched the night before, or the latest piece of gossip. Young people especially say they never tell or listen to stories, but when I begin to tell an Anansi or a Creation tale they hang on to every word.

I offer a fresh and vibrant approach to literature and language in the forms of storytelling, the oral tradition, creative writing, drama and reading development. I have been engaging with schools over twenty-five years, and I never get tired of the buzz that greets each visit... from children beaming with pride and sheer happiness as they perform their work in assemblies, to the child whose radiant smile lights up the world as they put the final touches to their poem or story.

I learnt 'on the job', and it was a real learning curve. Sometimes I had to stand my ground as a writer and storyteller, and insist I was not a substitute English teacher. These were lessons quickly learnt and ones maintained throughout all the years of working in schools. Relax, go with the flow, and your artform will prevail.

I am often asked: Where do I get my stories from? I read a lot. I do my research. I visit libraries and bookshops. I just love to read all kinds of books. And the internet has developed into a useful tool. Just key in the word *stories* and you get a wealth of information. And of course I write stories myself, and the ideas for these come from everywhere: objects, the sky, the sea, passing conversations... have imagination, will travel a long long way.

I also use Drama in my sessions - where the stories are played out. Recently I was telling stories to a Year 8 assembly and they wanted to act them out. Far from trying to be cool, they had a very good time. It was a chance to do something without inhibitions... a chance to laugh and play, to be that small child again.

Sandra Agard's work has been published by The Women's Press, and her play for children, *Abena's Stupidest Mistake*, was performed at The Drill Hall in London in 2004. Sandra is currently the Literature Development Officer at Peckham and New Cross Libraries in South-East London.

The Workshop

"All that planning – then the moment arrives when I walk into the classroom. 'This is it,' I say to myself, 'let's write!'"
Writer

During a school visit writers will read their work, answer questions and most will lead a workshop. For some teachers this word might conjure up an image of sawdust and nails, so here we describe some workshop structures, practicalities such as space and equipment, and ideas for creating your own exercises.

The space

As one project co-ordinator says, the most important thing the teacher can do is to create *"a space that is conducive to creativity, is comfortable and laid out so the children have room to think and write"*. Beyond their obvious physical significance, addressing issues of space and comfort gives a clear message that this activity is valued. Here we focus on a few things to consider when looking at suitable work spaces.

There are two ways to accommodate a writer's visit in the school: the writer can either be taken from class to class, or can stay in one place while groups are brought in turn. The latter works well for writers who prefer certain seating arrangements. Playwrights or poets may need the school hall for performance or rhythm exercises; others may request the computer suite or library. All these work spaces will probably need booking in advance. In primary schools younger children can use the 'carpet area', which provides an intimate and relaxed way to gather together for reading and group work. Open-plan areas and those with through-traffic are best avoided, and spaces without tables can make it hard to write... though a box of clipboards turns any space (indoors or out) into a writer-friendly zone!

The tools

A writing workshop is refreshingly simple to equip, but – especially in secondary schools – the teacher still needs to ensure pens and paper are available. Since most writers emphasise the importance of the drafting process, jotters or rough books are useful; as Alan Ziegler says in his book The Writing Workshop, *"students need to be reminded that neatness is not a virtue on a rough draft"*. Providing a flip-chart as well as a dry-wipe board means that scribed work can be saved, and the giant paper is useful when students work in groups. If IT equipment is required it's worth the teacher and writer checking it out before the session starts.

Refreshments don't quite qualify as equipment, but access to water is essential. Supplying the writer and students with a drink provides a natural focus for a break and avoids any dips in concentration from dehydration.

"My main objective as a writer is for young people to see creative writing as a valued and pleasurable activity. Anything the teacher does to make the workshop feel special helps make this happen."
Writer

The introduction
A good introduction improves the dynamic of any workshop or performance and puts the writer and the work into context. Teachers can prepare an introduction by jotting down a few lines from the writer's CV, book jacket or publicity material. If the writer prefers a specific introduction, make sure teachers have it in advance. This initial contact with the group or class is also an opportunity to check break times with the group and outline the activities. Pupils may know a writer is coming, but often have little idea of what is to happen. The first few minutes can be a lovely 'handshake moment', where the writer takes in the young people, and vice versa. Don't let it all be lost in a fluster of finding somewhere to put down coats and bags.

Both young people and adults need to feel safe to be creative. It's very common to feel nervous at first. In his book Jumpstart Poetry in the Secondary School, writer and teacher Cliff Yates emphasizes the power of the right atmosphere: *"The writing workshop is based on mutual respect; no one can write in a group which doesn't take this for granted, just as no pupil will do their best if they think what they say or write is not valued"*.

The activities
Writing exercises are the essence of the writer's toolkit. An inspirational writing exercise will spark ideas, encourage you to explore technique and address the important business of observation through the senses. By prompting young people to look at the world in a different way, a good writing exercise will teach what theory alone cannot.

Exercises can take the form of word-games, visual or sensory prompts, and samples of writing which act as models and frames. They often involve group and individual work. A workshop commonly starts with a warm-up – a short individual exercise, or perhaps a piece of group writing with someone scribing on the board. Simple and achievable, the warm-up offers a chance to get to know the pupils and reassure the group about expectations. It provides clues about the group's abilities and dynamics, while at the same time introducing a link into the main exercise. It gets the students focused, while establishing a relaxed workshop atmosphere; a warm-up can also be a calm-down.

The role of the workshop is to get pupils writing in limited time and under the artificial constraints of the exercise. These can feel like pressures, but they have a releasing effect. Ted Hughes described it like this: *"These artificial limits create a crisis, which rouses the brain's resources: the compulsion towards haste overthrows the ordinary precautions, flings everything into top gear, and many things that are usually hidden find themselves rushed into the open. Barriers break down, prisoners come out of their cells"* (Poetry in the Making).

Writers will need at least one 'Break this Glass in Case of Fire' exercise. This is a sure-fire hit that will win over the shy, the exuberant or the reluctant. Whether it involves humour, shock tactics or students lying on the floor composing a poem on what it's like to be dead, a BTGICOF might just save your life.

Reading, redrafting and reviewing students work
"I'm keen for the students to experience the disciplines of editing and redrafting as something other than red-pen slog. It's the manipulation of the core material of your craft, peeling away excess to reveal the shape of what's there."
Mandy Coe (Writing Together)

The group may all start writing at the same time, but while one pupil chews on a pencil wondering how to begin, someone else will put up a hand: "I'm finished!". It helps if the main exercise can be developed in some way, and this leads to the subject of redrafting.

With secondary pupils, group feedback (in groups of five or six) provides a chance for peer editing and a closer examination of each piece of writing. Sue Dymoke observes that pupils who make progress in their writing are *"learning to draft (and, in some instances, to work with a drafting partner)"* as well as *"learning to look critically at their own work and to accept constructive criticism from others"* (Assessing your pupils' poetry). Traditionally, students see redrafting as an unwelcome labour: "Do I *have* to write it out again?". But writers bring a more positive view. Revision is not simply the correction of errors; it is a continuation of the creative process. Here are a few points to be explored:

- Does the piece flow/make sense?
- Read it aloud to explore voice, rhythm or line breaks.
- Can the sequence/timeline be altered?
- Are opening and closing lines at the beginning or somewhere else?
- Is essential information missing? Or is the writer telling us too much?
- Is there accidental repetition or ambiguity?
- Can the piece be tightened by removing unnecessary words?
- Check the possibilities and consistency of viewpoint and tense.
- Is the piece to be reworked for display, using design or illustration?

Speaking after a Writing Together residency, Walkden High School teacher Rob Chisnell noted: *"The students' work has improved, they edit more efficiently, they're more confident creatively... Best of all they have learned to evaluate their own writing more effectively, rather than just checking in with the teacher"* (Times Educational Supplement).

Building in time to share students' work can be daunting. Hearing each student read aloud in a class of thirty takes up a big chunk of the workshop. However, young people love to read their work aloud and this is an invaluable chance for them to get feedback, gain peer recognition and enjoy being a live literature audience. Group performances can also be great fun. As one teacher explained after a workshop using group performance, *"the workshop was well structured. At first all together, then split into groups. It made them confident to express and perform their ideas"*.

Sometimes there is someone in the group who doesn't want to read out their work. This can happen in all workshop situations, with adults as well as young people. Situations like this need handling with sensitivity, but sometimes a little encouragement is all that's needed. Adrian Mitchell says: *"I don't force anyone to read, but I do say it's a bit like being on a football pitch, if the ball comes to you, it's only polite to kick it somewhere, even if you're not Ian Rush – yet. It's just a game, not a competition"* (There's a poet behind you).

Individual or group work
"On the one hand there are the children. On the other, there is the child. I walk into the classroom and I face the children, thirty at a time."
Philip Gross (The Poetry Book for Primary Schools)

Writing collaboratively with the whole class is a vibrant and exciting way to engage students. The sheer adventure and drive of it creates spectacular work, giving the class and the writer a feeling of achievement. This confidence helps young people of all abilities when they start writing individually. But the quieter ones – who don't respond to humour, or are slower to articulate an idea – can be lost in the rough-and-tumble of whole-class work, so a workshop that uses both methods is ideal.

Scribing for the whole class makes the drafting process visible. In stepping back from the discussion at certain points the writer can emphasise, summarise, or question what's being said. Because the writing is 'public property', students are liberated from feelings of attachment that might make them reluctant to cut unnecessary words or phrases. You can pool ideas, check for rhythm and pace or discuss the pitfalls of forced rhyme. It's not practical for the class to vote on every word, but if the thinking behind decisions is shared a balance can usually be found between democracy of input and the need to finish before nightfall!

Questions and answers

No author will spend the whole visit talking about himself. But at the other extreme, some writers fail to comprehend that their own experiences are a valid resource in the classroom. Through insecurity, shyness or fear of being seen to blow their own trumpet, the writer may assume the role of educator and let his or her identity *as a writer* become almost incidental. But why should schools fundraise to bring in a writer, when they have perfectly good English teachers? The writer's passions and experience must be integral to their work with young people, and another way of sharing these is through a question-and-answer session. If the very thought makes your mind go blank, here are a few subjects which pupils have raised with us and other writers:

- *What work space do you use?* Show photos of the office/kitchen table
- *How long does it take?* Two years to write that novel; the draft poems put away for months
- *Is every idea a good one?* How some avenues are really cul-de-sacs
- *What does it feel like to seek publication?* Rejection and acceptance slips are of particular interest – be brave and take some in!
- *Why is reading integral to the process of writing?*
- *How do you find and record ideas?* Show notebooks, copies of drafts
- *How is writing published?* Show samples of your published work. Use them to talk about the other roles involved: proof-readers, editors, illustrators, designers, etc.

Schools can prepare beforehand for question-and-answer sessions. The poet Sandy Brownjohn says: *"I think the most important thing is for writers to go into schools and read their work, talk about how they work and answer questions. What seems important here is that the school should prepare for the visits. Schools can make sure that they've read the work to the children, that they've talked about the poems and encouraged them to think of questions they want answered. Writers like this!"* (The Poetry Book for Primary Schools).

Preparation is a good idea, but don't underestimate the ability of your pupils to come up with their own form of words. When a 10-year-old girl asked John Agard "What did you want to be if you couldn't be in the poem business?" it inspired him to talk about the unpredictability of poetry writing: *"The poem business is not like Boots or Woolworths. The poem business doesn't have regular opening and closing hours. Just when you think you've closed up shop for the night and it's time to sleep, that's just when you might get a line or two, or even a whole poem, knocking at your door"* (There's a poet behind you).

38

Creating your *own* writing exercises

For some writers, their ways of working in the classroom are a private matter, and they want to keep their store of exercises secret or as their trademark. A writer's favourite exercise – about mini-beasts in space, or interviewing a Victorian button-hook – may represent a tried-and-tested method of unlocking the imagination. But for many writers it is pressure of time that keeps them using the same exercises over and over again. Writers who get work by recommendation can be understandably wary of trying out a new approach. It feels risky. But over time our workshop repertoire can become divorced from our passions as writers, and the real risk is in becoming stale.

"Among the emerging semi-professional caste of workshop leaders, animateurs and group workers of all kinds, we can get rather pleased with our 'own' stock of games and exercises. Hands up anyone who has really invented a good writing exercise, from scratch? The good ones are like folk songs, picked up and adapted, variation on the common stock. Can we admit that, without putting ourselves out of jobs?"
Philip Gross (Writing in Education)

This aspect of work in schools highlights a clear professional need for writers and teachers. Whether through teacher training, INSET or specific training for writers, both professions need opportunities to *design new exercises* as well as learn about existing ones. The techniques we use in devising new exercises deepen our understanding of the writing process and how it can be taught. This is a chance to consider the correlation between the way professionals write and the way we ask young people to write in the classroom.

Writers should not rule out using samples of their own writing. Those who do not write for children can feel at a loss as to what work is suitable for use in schools. But assuming the material is not wildly inappropriate, writers can extract and adapt a short sample to illustrate a certain technique, style, or theme. Ask another writer to look at your work with an eye to what might work for a particular age-group. Kit Wright, who writes for both children and adults, says: *"I often read poems to children that come from my adult collections"* (Young Writer). It's a mistake to assume that young people only respond to stories or poems written specifically for children. They don't.

"While there are some good poems which are only for adults, because they presuppose adult experience in their readers, there are no good poems which are only for children."
WH Auden

Some things to look for in your own work are: voice, narrative, use of dialogue, monologue, description, pace, secrets, memories, rhythm, pattern, character... A short extract can be typed out alongside a couple of bulleted points that highlight the specific features. For example: 'In this piece, Alan Jones uses monologue as a way of revealing the character's thoughts. Place *your* character in a challenging situation (on the wrong train, trapped in a lift, left to fly a plane), and using monologue, describe what happens.' Alan Jones can then leave this with teachers as a resource.

There are many books of writing exercises you can use and adapt (see *Further Reading* and *Websites*). Take a look at www.poetryclass.net (click on **Poetry lessons**) and www.applesandsnakes.org (**Resources**).

Inspiration! Resources in the classroom

The richest resource in any classroom is the pupils' imagination. The unconscious can be tapped by techniques such as 'automatic writing' or 'ink-wasting' (continuous writing about absolutely anything that pops into your head). The etymology of the word *inspiration* is "to breathe in", and for most writers the process of writing is not simply about writing. It is about *being*: being receptive to detail; looking, listening, feeling. This is a wonderful thing to teach young people. Everyone can benefit from the heightened awareness brought about by exploring internal and external worlds.

Objects and people

Bring in a pair of shoes, a hat, a stone, a bone. Speaking in the voice of that object, the pupil can explore its history and world view. This works not only with inanimate objects but with people: invite a guest into the classroom, let the teacher answer questions in character, or invent a character based on a photograph. Before students ask questions see how far they get with the 'silent interview technique' (gathering as much information as possible, just by observing). By bringing in resources that stimulate them to write, writers can share their own interests and passions.

Abstract exercises

Encourage young people to give their imagination free rein. Some students would sooner make an educated guess at a mathematical equation than try and answer the question 'What colour is a dog's bark?'. It takes courage to feel you are right when there is no wrong answer. A writer's reassurance that invention is allowed can be liberating. Sometimes, part-way into a workshop, a pupil will ask 'Do you mean I'm to *make it up*?' as if you have asked them to do something a little sinful. As well as interviewing an object, try interviewing an emotion such as *jealousy*, a subject like *peace* or a feeling such as *hunger*. Encourage pupils to write about big abstract ideas in vivid concrete terms.

Reading

Apart from reading for the sheer pleasure of it, texts can be used to prompt students' writing either as a **model** (an example of a specific theme, structure or technique), or as a **frame** (a more prescribed starting point or repeated pattern).

"When selecting models and planning how to teach them, try to ensure that the end results will not involve marking thirty almost identical poems. While it might be easier to compare the poems for assessment purposes it will not help pupils to develop as independent original writers and the marking will be very tedious! Allow time for exploration of ideas and layers of meaning of the poem as a whole rather than a quick ten minutes to soak up a template."
Sue Dymoke (Assessing your pupils' poetry)

Be sure the model is an example of excellent writing, rather than mediocre text that simply illustrates a form. Look out for pieces with certain features of voice, theme or structure. They might contain metaphor, simile, narrative, characterisation; they might use lists, questions, nonsense, unusual syntax; you might find a story told in a non-linear way. Pupils can also be asked to respond to the piece by exploring a different voice, an opposing view. Diary extracts, letters, monologues and reportage will all expand the range of their reading and writing. In time, you will find yourself looking at all kinds of text as a possible resource, and quickly accumulate a good collection of examples.

Talking freely

In his book Did I Hear You Write? Michael Rosen argues that the way young people talk should be reflected in the way they write. This applies to both language and content. Pupils should be encouraged to see their own vocabulary, phrasing and linguistic habits as valid tools for writing. A glance at any contemporary novel, play or poetry anthology reminds us that, although we all need literacy skills, we are limited neither to Standard English nor to grand themes. The use of dialect is fun and inclusive, and if a writer or teacher does need to give help or feedback on a dialect or phonetic piece, their role can be that of a translator checking for consistency and sound.

"She said she sometimes goes down to the park to listen to how kids talk to each other – you can tell that because when her characters talk in her books they sound real, quite like me and my mates sound."
Pupil

Creative writing is inclusive because its subject matter is to be found everywhere: in the wildest realms of the imagination, and in our homes and streets. Children who have never left their own district have as much to tell as those who are well travelled. Current events, local news, pupils' lives and observations will always provide a wealth of subject matter. As one writer told us:

"In one residency I asked a class for local news and we wrote about a pub fire at the end of the street. In a history lesson on the Vikings later that week they had asked the teacher how anyone knew what happened so long ago. 'Someone had documented it' she told them. 'What, the way did when we wrote about the fire Miss?'".

"That's the art of fantasy: showing people things from a new direction. Familiar objects – or people or beliefs – seen from a new direction can often be more 'fantastic' than anything an author could invent."
Terry Pratchett (Young Writer)

Images

As William Carlos Williams famously said: *"No ideas but in things"*. Photographs, posters and postcards can stimulate marvellous writing. Pictures are Alice-in-Wonderland doorways, leading out of the classroom and into other worlds. When we pass through them, what do we see, smell and touch? And doorways are entrances as well as exits; characters from pictures can also visit us.

Another approach useful in this age of technology is to think of the image as a video or DVD on Pause. By writing, the students are pressing Rewind, Fast Forward or Play. The poet Matthew Sweeney says: "I like in my poems to tell a story with a succession of images – like the way a film works, only this time the film is in words" (National Poetry Day booklet, 2004). One of the most useful things we can teach a young writer is that words can be used in the same way a camera can, to show a wider picture and to zoom in on specific detail. Good writing speaks not only to the ear, but also to the mind's eye. Readers or listeners should be able to shut their eyes and see the landscape, the characters, the detail.

Other languages

In Luna, Luna: Creative Writing ideas from Spanish, Latin American and Latino Literature, Julion Marzan encourages us to use Spanish words and phrases, whether or not we are Spanish speakers. Borrowing from another language can expand the potential of young people's writing. Try 'translating' a poem from an unfamiliar language by simply studying the shape and sound of the words. This is subject is explored further in *Languages*.

Listening

Writers are great eavesdroppers (and therefore notoriously bad company in pubs and cafes!). Pupils can be encouraged in the habit of noting the way people speak: turns of phrase, favourite words, verbal mannerisms or the odd juxtaposition of ideas. All of these are great triggers for writing.

"The starting point for a poem is very often a cliché or a set of words taken out of context. I remember my mother telling me that what made me laugh uncontrollably as a baby (before language, I think) was when she took a familiar object, eg a teapot, and put it in an unfamiliar place, eg on the mantelpiece... the world turned topsy-turvy."
Roger McGough (National Poetry Day booklet, 2002)

Working with early years

"The ideas younger children come up with are astonishing. I have been left speechless by the power of their imagery."
Writer

Schools can struggle to find writers willing to work with this age-group, and reception classes are often omitted from primary school residencies altogether. The sheer physical exuberance of a roomful of five-year-olds, twinned with their inability to write more than a few words, has reduced more than one visiting author to tatters. But the sureness of their world view, combined with a fierce confidence in metaphor and storyline, can result in stunning writing! There are few ways writers can gain confidence in this other than 'on the job', so ask for teacher support and have a go. The following points may help:

- use group work and scribing;
- keep workshops short – no longer than 20-30 minutes;
- have extra helpers;
- mix writing with short readings (group participation goes down well);
- use images and illustration.

"The basis of workshops is oral improvisation and word-play warm-ups. Young children are quicker on the draw with their mouths than in the pencil application department."
Andrew Fusek Peters (The Poetry Book for Primary Schools)

Timetabling

There is a remnant in all of us that responds to the school bell in a certain way: time to get working, or else! Co-ordinators usually leave the issue of timetabling to the teacher and writer, but teachers may find it hard to imagine any schedule other than the standard school day. On the phone, scribbling down a complex school timetable, the writer is in danger of agreeing to a day of fragmented workshops with no time allowed to change rooms or take a break. Of course it is up to the teacher and writer to finalise timetabling details together, but project co-ordinators can help enormously by advocating against daily schedules that leave the writer hoarse, dehydrated and exhausted.

Most writers work on the principle of two two-hour blocks in a day, and negotiate within that structure. Writers who work in schools know from experience that unfamiliar and often lengthy journeys during rush-hour can make you crazy, late or both, and most will recommend a slightly later start. It is important to conclude the session with enough time to tidy up and hand over to the teacher for the end-of-day chat on homework, etc. Here are some model timetables used by writers and schools. All of them can be adapted to accommodate break times or to suit the age-groups the writer is working with.

10am – 12pm
one hour lunch
1pm – 3pm

Simple and easy to remember, this basic structure can incorporate mini-breaks inside the classroom if needed. This day allows for two groups, half a day each; or four groups, 50 minutes each (allowing time to change classrooms). For those who need more substantial breaks, but who still want one-hour sessions, the following timetable may be better:

9.30 – 10.30
half hour break
11 – 12
one hour lunch
1 – 1.45
half hour break
2.15 – 3.15

Those who are working in Early Years will find shorter sessions (30 minutes) more suitable:

9.30 – 10.10
20 mInute break
10.30 – 11.10
20 mInute break
11.30 – 12
one hour lunch
1 – 1.40
20 mInute break
2 – 2.40

In a residency the timetabling will vary from day to day. The writer may want to take aside smaller groups within the classroom for 15 minutes each, or work with one class for a half or whole day. The Teachers & Writers Collaborative, which organises many hundreds of writers' residencies per year, suggests breaking the school day into four 'class periods'. During residencies they recommend working with three classes and using the fourth period for an activity of the writer's choice. This could be an interview for the school magazine, or meeting with pupils one-to-one in the library.

All of these are only suggestions. Writers must be flexible, but should still feel able to suggest a schedule of activities determined by their experience of what works best... not the demands of a rather loud bell.

Roles in the classroom

"Research carried out into the value of writers working in schools found that some of the most significant developments in pupils' attitudes and achievement came about in those classes taught by teachers who had watched a writer's workshop and interpreted it (a 'cascaded' model): the writer and teacher together made the difference."
(From Looking Glass to Spyglass)

Writers do not want to be confused with supply teachers. If they are confident in front of the class, it may seem acceptable for them to work without a teacher. A few writers even tell the school how experienced they are with young people and that they're happy to be left alone. But a teacher, preferably one familiar with the class, **must be present at all times**. This is not optional; legal and insurance requirements make it mandatory. The writer is a visitor, and that role is jeopardised if they are left in sole charge of the health, safety and discipline of a class.

Writers learn to beware the teacher who says "Just popping out for a bit..." then reappears in full PE kit saying "Don't mind if I referee the netball, do you?". This leaves the writer with three nightmare options. The first is panto (with pupils as fascinated audience): "I can't be left alone with the class." "Oh yes you can." "Oh no I can't..." The second is to get on with it, praying there are no injuries, fire alarms or fisticuffs. Option three is to leave the class unsupervised and chase the teacher down the corridor...

Thankfully, the majority of teachers are enthusiastic, welcoming, flexible and willing to be involved. If the writer responds positively, a good partnership springs up. In the words of Naomi Wilds, Literature Development Officer with Derby City Council, *"the teacher needs to feel empowered and enriched, engaged by having an artist in the class"*. Here are three possible roles the teacher can play during the session:

Observer: in certain circumstances it may make sense for the teacher to observe and make notes for professional development purposes. In an evaluation study of a residency in Manchester, one teacher noted that the writer's *"considered questioning technique and well organised tasks were invaluable to observe and have influenced my classroom teaching"*.

Assistant: if the workshop involves individual or group work, the writer might ask the teacher to assist individuals who find it difficult to write or stay on task. Simply by going round the room, giving positive feedback, the teacher is playing an invaluable role.

Participant: for many writers, the ideal is to have the teacher join in, on an equal footing: writing with the students and reading back to the group what they have written. This 'take no prisoners' approach is, for some, fundamental to the idea of the workshop. It can be a nervous prospect for teachers, but the courage of those who are prepared to do it demonstrates to young people that writing is valued, that it is something everyone can enjoy doing, and that it is equally challenging for all. Writer Ann Sansom says: *"I'd much rather have a teacher who is writing. If they're supervising, or watching, they're learning 'tricks', ways of making things happen in the classroom. They're missing most of it. And the benefit of the teacher writing with the children is immense because the teacher is seen to be vulnerable"* (Jumpstart Poetry in the Secondary School).

Negotiating these roles

"I hold no grudge against the teacher who said 'Do you mind if I clear out my stock cupboard while you're doing this?'. She was probably unsure what her role could or should be; we hadn't discussed it."
Writer

Ideally, writers and teachers will have met in advance, but on a one-day visit the first contact is usually at the classroom door, with a quick introduction and a handshake. "What would you like the children to call you?" the teacher whispers, and the session is up and running. The writer might automatically defer to the teacher (this is after all the teacher's domain), but meanwhile the teacher is deferring to the writer (who is after all an authority in this field). The teacher, having handed over the baton of the chalk, may feel surplus to requirements and tiptoe away to get on with something else.

But the teacher is a key player in the workshop. All the planning, the aims, the effort lead to this moment: the actual *doing* of the project. Students watch their teacher closely for cues on how to participate, and a withdrawal of enthusiasm and engagement can flatten the atmosphere, making a successful workshop that bit harder to achieve. As one writer puts it: *"My personal bugbear is teachers who sit at the back of your workshop marking books. This makes me feel like a performing seal, an irrelevance to the real work of the school, and makes me angry at the rudeness of the adult who feels they'll gain nothing from what I do".* The Literacy Trust states it quite clearly: *"Never leave an author alone with a class. If possible, take part in the session".*

Once the workshop is underway, it is courteous to be sensitive to the teacher's authority, routines and working methods. If a teacher has worked hard to establish good habits in spelling and the presentation of neat work, explaining that first drafts can be messy will be much more welcome than making a throwaway comment that 'spelling doesn't matter'.

Classroom management

A well-planned, lively workshop is usually novel and engaging enough to ensure better than average behaviour. On the odd occasion when problems do occur, it's the job of the teacher – who knows the class and has authority – to intervene. Most writers prefer an atmosphere that's more relaxed than the usual lesson, so the teacher – however eager to show the class in the best light – shouldn't jump in too heavily. But anarchy is another matter! If a session is dominated by those who can shout loudest, many pupils will be left out. Teachers have neighbouring classes to consider, and if the writer is intending to get some noisy audience participation going, or have pupils standing on tables to perform their poems, it's best to check this with the teacher in advance.

Looking after the writer

The following tips for a successful visit are drawn from questionnaire responses from writers. They range from planning issues to be dealt with in advance, to simple things to be done on the day. Nearly every writer mentioned the cup of tea!

Look after your writer: a checklist

- Nominate one teacher who has over-all responsibility for the writer throughout the project. Pass on contact details and convenient times to get in touch.

- Post or fax a map and directions well in advance.

- Reserve a space in the car-park, or direct the writer to safe on-street parking nearby.

- Book accommodation in a hotel with predictably good facilities. If you're thinking of arranging a stay in a teacher's home, check with the writer first. Some welcome it, but others prefer to take time out. One writer famously described the experience as "a one-night stand without the sex"!

- Organise availability of books in school, if appropriate.

- A few days before the visit, put up a notice or 'project poster' in the school staff-room with the writer's picture and details of the visit.

Look after your writer: a checklist (continued)

- The day before the visit, talk about the writer and remind pupils of what is to happen on the day.

- Meet and greet and offer a cup of tea. Introduce the writer to all the teachers he or she will be working with.

- Ensure the receptionist or 'greeter' shows the writer into the staff-room. One writer sums up a common experience: *"Everyone had their own teabags and nobody offered me one; there didn't seem to be any mugs for visitors"*.

- Make sure the writer is escorted from class to class.

- Reimburse travel expenses as they are incurred, rather than in one lump sum at the end which can leave the writer out of pocket.

- Either offer lunch or give directions to the nearest sandwich shop. Sometimes a school provides a special lunch for writer and teachers to share. This adds to the sense of occasion and is a great chance to chat informally. Check for dietary restrictions.

- Big up the writer! As Brian Moses puts it, *"if your children believe that your visitor is 'special' then the day's writing or poetry will be special too"* (Inviting a poet into your school).

- Parents will also be interested – how about a note home, including a few details and an invitation to come in half an hour before home-time to meet the writer?

- At the end of the day, make sure the writer is thanked appropriately and is shown out of the building. *"How many writers looking for the car park end up by the bins, with the Reception class waving through the windows?"* (Writer).

Inclusion

"Every child has a right to participate freely in cultural life and the arts."
(United Nations Convention on the Rights of the Child)

We know how painful it feels to be excluded as an adult, let alone as a child. Luckily there are plenty of things we can do, and organisations which offer support (See *Useful Organisations* and *Websites*).

Working in schools in Britain brings us into contact with children and young people with a broad range of abilities, as well as a huge variety of religious and cultural backgrounds. From the mill towns of Lancashire to the suburbs of London, the Shetland Isles to inner-city Birmingham or Glasgow, we find the vibrant cultural heritage on which creativity thrives. Exploring other languages and traditions provides a wealth of possibilities for our writing. The Centre for Studies on Inclusive Education recommends that we view the differences between students *"as resources to support learning, rather than as problems to be overcome"*. But many communities and their schools are also forced to live with the pressures arising from discrimination, and social and economic deprivation. The children's charity, Barnardo's estimates that one in four children in the UK is living in poverty. How might these factors affect our work with schools?

Before taking part in any project, children have to cross a number of barriers; to join in wholeheartedly they will face a few more. Confidence makes a real difference to levels of participation, and young people going through difficult life experiences may have lower self-esteem than others. If they have experienced negative stereotyping, or if their views have been ignored in the past, they are much less likely to be motivated to join in. In Michael Rosen's words, *"part of the business of being a child is being not-powerful"* (Did I Hear You Write?).

Teachers may be conscious of this when selecting who is to participate in the project. Most writers enjoy working with young people of all abilities and backgrounds, and we can all be surprised by which young people shine. This is one of the real rewards of the job. Writers know that a background of poor literacy skills and low academic expectations need not be a barrier to creative writing. Paul Munden writes that *"teachers began to realise that we could get some of the best work from the pupils who weren't seen as particularly gifted. Indeed, it is often those who are not academically motivated who benefit the most from the writer's different approach"* (Writers & Teachers).

Occasionally, a writer may be heard to suggest that there is a contradiction between *making writing accessible to all* on one hand and *striving for excellence* on the other. Perhaps they think that by encouraging everyone to 'have a go', we could mislead people into thinking it's easy. This might reflect an understandable wish to protect the hard-won status of professional writers, and to gain recognition for skills and expertise acquired over the years.

But we writers cannot claim a monopoly on the activity of writing; it is a birthright and belongs to everyone. By choosing to get involved in education work we are reaffirming what Alan Gibbons calls *"the notion of writing as an essentially democratic impulse, something that anyone can do and everybody should try"*.

We strongly advise all those working in writers-in-schools projects to develop their own code of good practice concerning inclusion and equal opportunities. Organisations should monitor and regularly review their policies, keep abreast of current good practice, access and provide training. But for the individual writer, reading this at the dinner table while Coronation Street blasts out from the living-room, it can feel a strange thing to do: "Turn that TV down; I'm developing a code of good practice!" It's tempting to leave it up to someone else. Responsibility for these issues should be negotiated between schools, writers and project co-ordinators. The following questions should be considered in planning the project, be monitored as it progresses and form part of the final evaluation:

Equal Opportunities: a checklist

- Do the children or young people understand what the project is about and what their role is? Did they have any say in its planning and in the selection of participants?

- Does the project consider the best interests of the child during every stage of planning? Are safety and access issues being addressed?

- Have writers been informed beforehand of any particular needs any of the children may have?

- During sessions, can everyone hear properly, and see the writer and the whiteboard clearly?

Equal Opportunities: checklist (continued)

- Do children who have any kind of disability have the necessary support within the school so that they can participate fully? This may involve pre-planning on access/mobility issues, use of special equipment and the presence of support staff.

- Not all children join in at the same levels – do activities contain a mixture of individual and whole-group work so as to encourage maximum participation?

- Does the session make use of a variety of learning styles (visual, auditory, kinaesthetic), so that all pupils are engaged?

- Are writers and co-ordinators countering the expectation that they might only want to work with the 'brightest' or 'most able' children?

- Is everyone involved aware of the requirements of legislation and of current good practice guidelines on inclusion and equal opportunities?

- Do the activities take into account cultural and language differences within the group?

- How is the group to be managed so that less dominant voices are heard and valued equally?

Special Educational Needs (SEN)

Children and young people who have learning difficulties are officially said to have 'Special Educational Needs'. Their difficulties may be a result of physical or sensory disability, an emotional or behavioural problem or developmental delay. Whenever possible, children identified as having special needs (and there are some who slip through the net) are educated in mainstream schools, with extra help from specialist teachers and teaching assistants. For children with acute special needs there are Special Schools. Under the 1994 Code of Practice, a Register is kept of all children who are a cause for concern; these children go through a process which may lead eventually to 'Statementing'. The Statement legally entitles the child to professional help appropriate to individual needs. Young people with special needs can experience a huge range of difficulties, including dyslexia, dyspraxia, attention deficit disorder or hyperactivity, and physical disabilities and medical conditions such as visual or hearing impairment, speech problems, epilepsy, eczema, asthma, cystic fibrosis, diabetes, Down's syndrome, muscular dystrophy, cerebral palsy, heart disease or renal failure.

Beware: the terminology used in this field is transient and quickly goes out of date. In any case, writers usually prefer to work with no preconceptions about individual pupils. But it is useful to have a basic understanding of what teachers are talking about, especially when making provision for inclusion.

It is always best to see young people as individuals, and start by listening to what *they* have to say. Children express it brilliantly in the 13 statements included in the Children's Charter (Scottish Executive 2004). The statements are taken from young people and directed to the adults who work with them:

• *Get to know us* • *Speak with us* • *Listen to us* • *Take us seriously* • *Involve us* • *Respect our privacy* • *Be responsible to us* • *Think about our lives as a whole* • *Think carefully about how you use information about us* • *Put us in touch with the right people* • *Use your power to help make things happen*
• *Help us be safe.*
(Creating Safety)

The United Nations Convention on the Rights of the Child states that children and young people have the right to express their views on all matters affecting them. Participation in the arts is one way of ensuring this right is implemented. As professor and author Jackie Royster puts it: *"The very act of writing, especially for people who do not occupy positions of status and privilege in the general society, is a bold and courageous enterprise"*.

So far we have looked at the experiences of young people, but there are related issues that affect practitioners in this field. Writers come from all religious and cultural backgrounds, and offer young people positive role models. After all, if young people cannot see themselves in a world they aspire to, they may believe they are not entitled to a place in it. But because an author is from a particular cultural community, it does not automatically follow that he or she will 'do rap', teach children Chinese calligraphy, come to school dressed in a particular costume or talk about slavery and emigration. Such stereotyping can be painful for writers, and especially distorting for those just starting out, who may feel pressurised to deliver.

Disabled writers may find it useful to contact their Arts Councils for the latest information about specific resources, and the National Disability Arts Forum has a useful website with numerous resources and links: www.ndaf.org. Some organizations, such as Graeae Theatre Company, writernet and NAWE, have run targeted programmes including training seminars and mentoring schemes. They continue to be active in this area as part of Creative Renewal, a programme exploring innovative solutions to countering discrimination in the labour market and funded by the European Social Fund under the Equal community initiative. NAWE has explored ways in which disabled writers can benefit from working in schools online. Using specially developed software, this is already proving an attractive option for writers who find it difficult to make actual visits to schools but who are keen on undertaking such work from their own premises and within a flexible schedule.

Excluded   *Andy Croft*

Going into schools these days is a complicated business. You are expected to be entertaining *and* funny *and* accessible. You are often there so that the school can show it has taken steps to address problems identified in the last OFSTED report, and to help the school promote itself in the local paper. You are required to help deliver the national Literacy Strategy, and more often than not to address issues like bullying, drugs and racism. You are supposed to help raise levels of self-esteem, especially among working-class children. You are expected to inspire reluctant male readers to pick up a book and enjoy it. You are somehow supposed to legitimise the world of books. And if all that were not enough, these days poetry must do its bit to tackle issues of social exclusion.

It's an impossible task, of course. Not least because poets and poetry have done so much to make people feel that they are excluded from the world of literature, creativity and poetry, that most books are written by and for and about other kinds of people. 'Exclusion' is a description of social and economic inequality, a delicate New Labour euphemism for what used to be known as Class. But it is also a measurement of cultural power. It's all very well to assert that literature belongs to everyone. But that's probably not how it feels if you are a 'reluctant male reader', a student with learning difficulties, a pupil excluded from mainstream schooling or in a Young Offenders' Institution.

And yet the need to express ourselves in the best words we can think of is a common human need. Not many children are wholly excluded from language. Most are fluent speakers of at least one register, which they can employ with subtlety and vivid power. English poetry, of course, chose a long time ago to exclude itself from the common music of common speech. But to describe those who find contemporary poetry unexciting, obscure and meaningless as 'excluded' is like that legendary headline in *The Times*, 'Fog in the Channel : Europe Cut Off'. Perhaps poetry could do with being a little less exclusive.

Moreover, poetry has only been written down in the last few hundred years. For most of human history it was mostly anonymous, public and shared, passed on and learned and changed and passed on again. Rhythm, metre and rhyme help listeners to memorise a poem and to be simultaneously the creators of its common music. It is only with the recent emergence of mass-literate societies in the West that art has become identified with the private expression in books of individual feeling. The power of all art is still located in society - in the audience and not in the artist. Kids somehow know this. It informs the rejection of the world of books as 'posh'. Young Offenders who improvise rap at the windows understand that you don't have to be able to write in order to write. You certainly don't have to be 'good at English' to write poetry.

Wherever possible, then, I use improvised, rhythmical, rhyming, whole-class writing games (not necessarily even written down). Poetry is both familiar and unfamiliar, recognisably strange and strangely recognisable, a democratic creative act that is equally hard and equally easy for everyone. Ask most children to write a story and the results will be unremarkable. But poetry has special musical rules - rhythm, rhyme, echo, alliteration, stanza, shape, diction etc - which won't let you reach for the first word that comes into your head. You have to attend to the rules of the game. Your words have to fit the pattern. You have to become a writer.

It can be a laugh. It can encourage the self-conscious use of heightened, patterned, musical language. It can assert the collective, shared ownership of poetry. It can develop a sense of the magic of words, a feeling for the unsuspected power and pleasure of using language with economy and precision. Above all, it involves a degree of ownership over 'writing' which makes its users more than simply consumers, gives them squatters' rights at least. It might even make them feel included, not in some stakeholder dream of student loans and private health insurance, but in the shared, common humanity out of which all art is made. Poetry included.

Andy Croft's books of poetry include *Nowhere Special, Just as Blue, Great North* and *Comrade Laughter*. He has also written thirty-four books for teenagers, mostly about football. With Adrian Mitchell, Andy has edited an anthology of British socialist poetry, *Red Sky at Night*. He has worked in over a hundred schools.

Good practice

Elements of good practice covered so far include:

- careful choice of writer;
- thorough planning;
- preparation with pupils;
- well designed activities;
- age-appropriate material;
- high-quality content;
- effective delivery;
- proper procedures;
- inclusion;
- evaluation and dissemination.

Good practice also means engaging with a range of ethical and legal issues around work with young people. Here we outline some of the essential things to be considered in the planning of any project, and explain how to find out more.

INTERVIEWS

For longer-term residencies an interview should be carried out. Ideally this will be face-to-face, but if the writer lives a long distance from the school it may have to take place by telephone. The interview is an opportunity not only to find out more about the writer's work but also to explore his or her previous experience of working with children and young people. Schedule interviews well in advance to allow time to think through any concerns that may arise at this stage.

REFERENCES

It is good practice for the writer to provide details of two referees who have agreed to be contacted. Referees should be people who know the writer's work *with young people.*

CHILD PROTECTION

It is possible that during your work with young people you may find yourself being confided in by a troubled young person. We are all under a legal responsibility to handle this correctly. For comprehensive guidance on this and other child protection issues, we recommend two publications:

- *Keeping Arts Safe: protection of children, young people and vulnerable adults involved in arts activities* (Arts Council England/ NSPCC)
- *Creating Safety: child protection guidelines for the arts* (Scottish Arts Council/Children in Scotland)

Both guides are available free of charge; for information see the Arts Councils' websites (listed at the back of this book).

DISCLOSURE

A Disclosure is a document containing information held by the police and government departments. It is used by employers and voluntary organisations to make safer recruitment decisions about people working with children, young people or vulnerable adults. There are two types of Disclosure: Standard or Enhanced. It is good practice for anyone working closely with young people to have Enhanced Disclosure.

The Disclosure system is complex. The summary here gives general guidance, correct at the time of going to press, but the system is frequently revised and updated, and all parties should seek detailed advice from the Criminal Records Bureaux which manage the Disclosure Service:

England and Wales	www.disclosure.gov.uk
Scotland	www.disclosurescotland.co.uk
Northern Ireland	www.dhsspsni.gov.uk

It is the **responsibility of the employer** (school or organisation) to make sure that every writer it employs has a Disclosure check. If the writer is contacted through a reputable organisation, Disclosure may already have been carried out. If not, time must be built into the planning of the project to allow the process to be completed – it can take up to three months.

An individual writer can apply for the check to be carried out only through a 'registered body' (an organisation officially registered with the CRB). The Disclosure service websites list these registered bodies, and individuals can contact them until they find one willing to process the application. We recommend that writers get in touch with NAWE, one of the organisations listed. NAWE processes Disclosure checks on behalf of all the writers and artists featured on its online database www.artscape.org.uk.

It's important to be clear that, even after receiving Enhanced Disclosure, **the writer should not be left alone with children or young people, individually or in groups**. Schools and project organisers are responsible not only for the protection of children but also for ensuring that writers are not placed in situations where abuse might be alleged.

Disclosure **is not a guarantee**. It is limited in scope, and it can only check a person's past record. There is no legal definition on how long it remains current; the onus is on employers to satisfy themselves that checks are relevant and up to date. Disclosure is a national certificate, but since employers have legal responsibility for the safety of young people in their care, it is up to them to decide whether an existing check is sufficient or whether to ask for a new one.

SCHOOL POLICIES

Each school has its own systems and procedures, and visiting writers should find out what they are and comply with them. Going back to school as an adult can bring out the rebel in some of us, but it's important to recognise that there are good reasons for the procedures schools put in place.

Signing in and out and being asked to wear a name badge is not an annoying bit of bureaucracy but a way of safeguarding children.

Photographs or film of pupils on or off school premises cannot be taken without prior discussion with the school. Most schools now have their own policies regarding images, which the writer must follow. Similarly, if pupils' work is to be broadcast or published (whether in print or on the internet), the school must be consulted about the use of their names. Schools are responsible for protecting young people from being identified in ways which might make them vulnerable.

Physical contact with pupils is to be avoided. While everyone knows that striking, pushing or shaking a child is completely outlawed, some may not be aware that hugging, ruffling hair or making affectionate physical contact of any kind is also inappropriate. Whether or not the writer agrees with this rule or understands the need for it is irrelevant. Visiting artists often find that some children are drawn to them and seek out physical attention; try to find imaginative ways of discouraging children from sitting on your lap, holding your hand and cuddling you by offering them alternatives such as sitting next to you, being a special helper, etc. If you feel in any way uncomfortable about the behaviour of a young person, discuss it with the teacher.

Smoking is now completely banned on most school premises.

Staff toilets only should be used by visiting adults.

INSURANCE

It is very important that writers working in schools are suitably covered in case of any accident for which they could be held liable. Local Education Authorities cover teachers and other employees of schools, but individual artists may need their own cover. Public Liability Insurance (PLI) to a minimum of £2 million cover is advisable.

If you are working for a small organisation, it may have insurance to cover you. But most writers freelance in a number of different contexts, and need to take out their own policy. Insurance is an important professional requirement, should be built in to the writer's annual overheads, and is tax-deductible. Many LEAs and other organisations now have a policy of employing only writers with PLI.

We recommend that writers contact NAWE for further information and advice on finding suitable insurance providers.

TEACHER PRESENCE

Many child protection issues are covered by making sure that **a teacher is present at all times while the writer is with pupils**. This stipulation is a core requirement of good practice, but schools often fail to take it seriously enough. The teacher is late, is absent, or is 'just popping out'. There is staff illness and the school 'can't get cover'. While we understand that teachers are under pressure, that flu spreads quickly amongst school staff, and that supply teachers are difficult to find in some areas, these problems are for the school to solve, and must not be dealt with by using the visiting writer to cover. Where there are staff shortages in school, it's best to arrange cover elsewhere and re-arrange teachers' timetables so that the writer is working alongside a teacher who knows the students and the school well. One writer told us: *"This teacher shrugged every time I asked a question. 'I don't work with this class,' she said"*.

Teaching assistants Sometimes writers find themselves accompanied by a teaching assistant rather than a teacher. Teaching assistants (also known as classroom assistants or learning support assistants in some areas) may be attached to a whole class, or may support one child or a small group of children with special educational needs. They are there to help teachers, and can be an extremely valuable source of support during a writer's visit. It is, however, bad practice to ask a teaching assistant to act as the 'teacher presence' in place of the class teacher. It leaves the writer – and potentially the school – in a vulnerable position with its insurers and the law.

Higher Level Teaching Assistants This is a new role with added responsibility. HLTAs still work under the direction and supervision of qualified teachers, but their duties can include working as a specialist assistant for a subject or department, contributing to lesson planning or developing support materials, or even supervising a class. This initiative is linked to Workforce Remodelling, part of the National Agreement on Raising Standards and Tackling Workload, signed in January 2003. One of the aims of this agreement is to give all teachers guaranteed non-contact time for planning and preparation. Supervision of a writer's visit by an HLTA rather than a teacher may fulfil legal requirements, and if the HLTA knows the class well the writer may not notice the difference.

However, best practice is for the class teacher to be present, participating and taking advantage of professional development opportunities offered by the session.

We have heard it suggested that Workforce Remodelling may open up 'opportunities' for writers and other artists to take sole charge of classes. *This is a retrograde step.* We would not welcome any blurring of the roles of writer and supply teacher. No amount of training in 'classroom management' changes the fundamentals of good practice.

Beyond the school: museums and galleries

From our feedback it is clear that some of the best projects schools have experienced with writers have taken place not *in* schools but *out of* them. Working in arts and heritage venues is a joy. In a gallery, the writer is immediately joined by a whole team of artists through the medium of their work. In a museum, the narratives that exist within and around objects beg for a creative response. Any trip out of school raises logistical issues, such as transport and staff cover. A risk assessment might have to be carried out by teachers or staff at the venue. But don't let this outweigh the benefits.

Here are a few examples of collaborations between schools and publicly funded bodies:

- A local authority Arts for Health project wants its healthy living campaign to include primary schools through a public performance in a local theatre. A writer is booked to go in to the schools and help devise a script.
- A concert hall wants schools to visit and would like a hands-on activity to be part of the experience. A writer is asked to come in a run workshops for them.
- A museum intends to interpret an exhibit with contributions from young and old in the community. The resident writer is asked to work with groups from the local school, responding to material produced in reminiscence sessions with senior citizens.

In each of these instances, the writer is being asked to work within a theme, and the project's success depends on communication between a number of individuals and organisations. Communication within hierarchical organisations like museums and schools is like communication within a small town. One simple way to address this is to design a project poster which can go up in staff-rooms, classrooms and public areas. Give the project a name, make it visual and make it sound fun. A project poster can:

- advertise the end result/event;
- show dates of project sessions;
- name the organisations involved;
- list the contact person at each venue;
- include name and photo of the writer.

Planning

Writers working in a gallery or museum will welcome at least one extra day built in to the initial costs. This time to visit the venue and plan is as important as the contact time with the students; it's a chance to become familiar with floor plans, exhibits and work spaces suitable for the day.* It's also a valuable opportunity to develop specific exercises and adapt ideas to suit the environment. These exercises, combined with postcards of artworks or artefacts, can be used later on with the whole school.

"The way in which the pupils used artwork as a source of inspiration has also given me ideas for future creative exercises. I may yet use the techniques practised at the gallery with a GCSE group for the creative writing element for the course."
Rob Chisnell, teacher (Writing Together)

Resources
If the work to be focused on during the day can be viewed on a website, or is reproduced in gallery guides, posters or postcards, it can be used for follow-up work back at school. Museums also have collections of objects that can be handled during educational work. It is worth asking what is available, as touch, smell and sound can greatly enhance creative work.

Work space
Time will be spent in public areas, but the school can often book the use of designated workshop space through the education department.

Staffing
Trips out of school are subject to a minimum ratio of staff to children, and extra help should be welcomed. The writer needs to know in advance how many staff will be present, for planning how to divide groups when required.

Setting the mood
Prepare pupils with information about the venue, exhibition and writer. Encourage them to explore relevant web sites or virtual galleries. Introduce them to the role of the Information Assistants; not only are they experts on particular exhibits but they will help anyone who gets lost. For some, this will be their first experience of visiting a museum or gallery, and the temptation to touch exhibits, or explore the joys of a slippery floor may be strong. It's good to start with an exercise that slows everyone down and gets them looking, listening, adjusted to the quieter, slower pace of this environment.

Timing
End the session in plenty of time for students to gather bags and coats, visit the shop and make their way to the coach. Everything is a bit more of an adventure in an unfamiliar venue: toilet breaks, drinks, lunch... Build this in to the schedule and remember many public buildings do not open their doors until 10 am.

* Exhibits can change and artworks are occasionally removed for cleaning or loan. Don't forget to check with the staff which artworks will be on display during the visit.

Refreshments

The British weather is unreliable, so identify alternative spaces indoors and out where packed lunches can be eaten. *Plenty of water must be available.* Galleries and museums can be airless and warm, and children who become dehydrated can very quickly feel ill.

Equipment

Clipboards may be available at the venue, allowing students to work in any indoor or outdoor space. The school should supply paper and pens.

Group sizes

Groups of more than 15 are problematic. In a gallery or museum, class-sized groups will be struggling to gather round the writer, see the artwork or find a space to write. In public areas, consideration must be shown to the visiting public, and in instances where young people are working on the floor they must not block entrances, exits or routes through the gallery. It is not ideal for writers or teachers to have to raise their voices to reach the group, as this can be intrusive for other visitors. Schools who want to expand the project to involve more pupils can take the new work back into school, share it in assembly, make a display using postcards or posters. Perhaps the project can become an annual event. As one teacher said of a project in a gallery: *"We had such good fun at the Tate. We made a huge display in school and now the year below is looking forward to their turn"*.

Partnerships

Partners are on the same team, working together to achieve shared aims. They should be clear about the shape of the project and what it's meant to achieve. Roles should be well-defined, so that all partners know where their responsibilities begin and end. That way, they won't be duplicating, treading on one another's toes or missing out important elements altogether.

WRITER AND SCHOOL

Jonathan Davidson, who has brought many schools and writers together under the Write On scheme, urges *"complete honesty and understanding between writer and school, especially about what is expected of both parties".*

Partnering the whole school 'The school' is a complex community of pupils, teachers, parents, governors and non-teaching staff. Writers should aim to partner the whole school, not just individual teachers. Establish friendly relations, right from the start, with non-teaching staff, so that they are aware of your presence and your work. Some school staff work in 'background' roles which are vitally important. The receptionist is the school's gatekeeper, an important ally in opening and maintaining channels of communication, passing on phone messages and email and providing expert help when the photocopier jams. Caretakers too are key people, and you'll be glad you made the effort to get to know them when you need heating turned up or down, doors unlocked or extra tables brought in. As for cooks and lunchtime supervisors, any writer who has ever worked with pupils in the school hall knows how important it is to have their co-operation and goodwill.

School librarians School librarians have valuable expertise in promoting literacy and literature. In fact, a librarian is often the dynamic force behind a writer's visit, and may have experience of booking and hosting events before. A key partner in both preparation and follow-up, the librarian can also provide resources to support the visit, including books, scripts, audio and video tapes. The library provides a safe place for students to read and write, and a space which can be used for cross-community partnerships, display and performance.

In the Times Educational Supplement, Kate Aldrich, head of English at Ludlow C of E Secondary School, and Susan S'ari, school librarian, write: *"When Children's Laureate Michael Morpurgo came the cost was shared between the school library and the Assembly Rooms. We always budget for at least one author a year from the library and English capitations".* (Susan S'ari also describes their annual Readers Award scheme: a boy and a girl from each year group are awarded a certificate and book prize based on book borrowing records from the school library.)

Understanding each other Each partner should be playing to his or her strengths: the writer devising the content of workshops and performances, and the teacher taking the lead in thinking through the pedagogical implications of the work. Good partnerships are built on mutual respect. As writers, let's recognise that we are lucky to be able to spend time in the classroom without having to deal with all the day-in, day-out realities of the teacher's working life. This leaves us free to occupy a different role: that of friendly adult showing the young people a good time on a different, less predictable activity.

There's no need for writers to caricature school as a rigid, repressive place where young people are force-fed arithmetic and grammar until a writer storms in to unlock the captive imagination. Naomi Wilds says that *"the writer needs to be 'literate' in school curriculum issues and classroom management style, so they don't undermine any procedures the teacher has put in place, but also take advantage of a more relaxed 'teaching' style as a visiting artist".*

"I've seen some stunning work done [in schools] and it just emphasises how I feel about teachers today, they're just fantastic and compared to teachers I had at school are just amazingly creative."
David Almond

If a project has gone particularly well, a writer may choose to write a letter to the Head giving positive feedback. This brings well-deserved recognition for hard work undertaken by individuals in the school community.

CO-ORDINATOR
Other projects involve a third partner: a literature or arts organisation, or a co-ordinator or literature development worker employed by the local council or libraries service. The small organisations we are talking about here are non-profit-making, often registered charities, doing marvellous work on shoestring budgets. In Scotland, many projects are initiated by Cultural Co-ordinators, whose remit is to broaden the range of cultural activities available to young people. These individuals and organisations have as part of their remit the brokering of collaborative work between schools and writers. They may work in a *reactive* way, responding to requests from schools, or in a *proactive* way, developing project ideas of their own, raising funds and approaching schools to take part.

It can be immensely helpful to have a third party involved. They can mediate between school and writer, and help resolve any problems that may arise. They can take some of the burden of administration from hard-pressed teachers. It's not always an entirely smooth ride; there can be moments of uncertainty about who is in charge of what (for instance, who has the purse-strings, who should the invoice be made out to, and why has the writer been quoted two different fees?). At the other extreme, the 'co-ordinator' is nowhere to be found, neither visits the project nor phones the writer to see how it's going. But literature development workers are highly creative people – very often writers themselves – and small literature organisations are treasure-houses of expertise. The best ones are real innovators. We should be making full use of their resources.

Brokering Triangular partnerships are very varied in the way they work. Sometimes the organisation or co-ordinator takes the lead: generating and researching ideas for projects, bringing all parties together and facilitating the planning process. Others act like dating agencies: taking requests, matching school and writer, passing on phone numbers and leaving them to make their own arrangements. This matching can be precise or clumsy.

Where organisations have a number of writers on their books, they use their knowledge and experience of each to choose the best fit. Problems arise if the most suitable writer is not available, and the co-ordinator – increasingly desperate to fulfil the booking – goes on down the list, phoning writers and getting no reply, until at last finding someone in. As one writer puts it: *"When the only thing the project wants to know is if I am free to work on that date, I know I'm going to have to pull the whole thing off with little or no support"*. Like so many problems, this one can be minimised by educating schools to start the process longer in advance. Last-minute requests are simply a bad idea.

Good co-ordinators are open and transparent in the way they select writers for jobs and how rates of pay are set. An atmosphere of openness is vitally important; organisations wield economic power over the writers on their books, and writers need to feel free to raise issues affecting their work in schools without jeopardising future employment prospects.

Know your writers One project co-ordinator hits the nail on the head when she says that she would like to *"have more knowledge of individual writers' styles of work in order to be able to match schools and writers more effectively"*. Where an organisation works with a pool of writers, it's essential that they know them all well, are properly familiar with their work and prepared to present them appropriately to schools. Organisations should make a policy of valuing the *artistic* careers of artists who work in schools. Otherwise, writers working for an organisation can feel like interchangeable 'units', sold to schools in a rather anonymous fashion, and in danger of becoming 'career workshoppers'. We prefer to be promoted complete with our personalities, please: our writing styles and histories, and our preferred ways of working with young people.

Many co-ordinating organisations do not specialise in education work, but have it as part of a wider remit which might include festival programming, reader development, work in prisons and so on. It can be a tall order for them to get to know each writer individually. Writers can help by supplying photographs, bibliographies, quotes and samples of work, giving co-ordinators a clearer picture of who they're putting forward. When good information is passed on to the school, it affirms that what they are buying is not some 'off-the-peg' package but *a special relationship with an individual writer*.

ROLES PROJECT CO-ORDINATORS CAN PLAY

- **Brief the writer** A certain amount of planning often happens before the writer is brought in. In this case the writer needs to be made fully aware of the aims of the project. Writers should see the wording of any initial meetings or funding proposals. They shouldn't go to a job knowing nothing more than venue, date and group size.

- **Act as a sounding-board** Rather than waiting to be asked, they can put themselves forward, encouraging both school and writer to talk through ideas and plans.

- **Build a profile of each writer** Not just the basics of age-groups and genres, but also comments and commendations from past projects. Writers should be asked to help keep records up to date by passing on news of recent successes.

- **Cheer the project on** Both school and writer will appreciate having a champion, who attends the performance or exhibition, writes a foreword for the anthology, visits the project, photographs and documents the work, etc. An occasional phone call to the writer to see how it's going is another valuable form of support.

- **Keep aims achievable** Avoid leaving the writer alone with unrealistic demands or unfeasible working conditions. Conscious of the need to secure more work in future, a writer can feel under pressure to manage difficult situations alone, but this is not good practice. Create an atmosphere where problems can be raised, discussed and resolved openly.

- **Be ready with Plan B** Where possible, there should be a back-up plan in case the writer has to drop out because of illness or other unavoidable circumstances. An organisation working with a pool of writers might offer a *suitable* alternative and, if a thorough paper-trail has been laid, will have all the necessary information at its fingertips, ready to pass on.

- **Co-ordinate and attend evaluation meetings** Not just at the end of the project, but throughout. In general, evaluation is the most poorly resourced and considered part of the project, but the co-ordinator can make sure it is funded, written up and fed into the planning of future projects. The wheel need not be reinvented each time.

- **Make policy on behalf of writers** For instance, guidance on how much non-contact time should be spent on a project. Day visits may need less time, but they still benefit from planning and preparation work within the school. Processing bookings simply by swapping contact details leaves the writer feeling responsible for everything else. Writers in this position will learn by 'coping' rather than supported development, particularly in the case of longer-term residencies.

- **Advise on funding** Co-ordinators can help schools gather information and fill out forms. An after-school funding advice seminar will prove popular with lots of schools in the area.

- **Take the lead on good practice** There is often the need for a third party to speak up loud and clear on issues such as Disclosure and teacher presence. Co-ordinators can send simple, accurate, current information to schools and writers as part of the booking or enquiry process.

- **Offer training and professional development** We discuss this topic further in *Writers: keeping the balance*. Co-ordinating organisations can be innovators in this field and make a real impact on the quality of project work.

- **Network with others** Contact between co-ordinators allows everyone to learn from each other. Sometimes organisations behave as though they are in competition, but the reality is that there is more than enough work to go around and that we can all afford to share experience. Co-ordinators who actively encourage writers to work with other projects benefit by those writers developing new professional skills, ideas and contacts.

- **Keep up to date** All small organisations need to be wary of the danger of getting 'stuck in a rut', doing things the way they've always been done regardless of changing circumstances. The best co-ordinators are the ones who invest in their own professionalism by reading, going to conferences and talking to others in the field so that they are aware of new developments.

Time for teachers

"The creativity of teachers needs to be more widely recognised, supported and nurtured, and their knowledge enhanced and regularly refreshed."
(From Looking Glass to Spyglass)

Writers cannot claim a monopoly on creativity. Teachers are creative people too – it's an essential ingredient of the job.

It's surprising how many teachers are themselves writers. In one year, 49% of applicants for Arts Council England writers' awards had taught at some level in the education system. Children's writers who started their careers as teachers include Eoin Colfer, David Almond and Philip Pullman. Other writers pay tribute to the role exceptional teachers played in their development. The novelist Andrew O'Hagan is one: *"I am a writer whose first mentor was a good teacher. We had no books at home, but at school I found a teacher who loved literature and loved writers: she made me want to be a good reader, and my whole life has followed from that"* (Writing Together).

Teaching is a high-pressure job, and the creative elements are often inadequately supported. As Chris Jones found during writing workshops with teachers: *"English teachers in secondary schools were particularly frustrated by having no time to engage in the vital creative aspects of their specialist subject, especially as they had chosen to teach English through a love of creative writing and reading"* (Poetry, Prose and Playfulness for Teachers and Learners).

Not all teachers are confident when it comes to creative writing. This is acutely true of poetry. Like many other adults, they may have been put off poetry by poor experiences at school or college, where it was presented as a dry academic exercise or a secret language. This fear or awe of poetry hinders the teaching of it. The practice of writers visiting schools has become so well-established that the poles have reversed and in some schools the pupils like poetry but the teachers don't.

There has been a growing trend over the past few years for literature organisations to 'build in' to their school projects an element of In-Service Training (INSET) and/or workshops for teachers. Writing Together, NAWE and other forward-looking organisations are placing it at the heart of their work with schools, and reporting real benefits for teachers and students. As one writer says, *"I no longer undertake longer-term residencies without some element of INSET. How can you hope to leave a positive legacy if you've left teachers out of the equation?"*.

Work with teachers should not be at the expense of encounters between writers and young people; the two are mutually supportive and our schools need both. Teachers are enthusiastic about INSET and writing workshops. In practice, however, schools do not always make them a priority. This quote from a project evaluation report will raise a wry smile of recognition amongst writers and co-ordinators: *"A focused writing workshop for teachers was also planned but due to difficulties in timetabling and availability none of the participating schools were able to take up this opportunity successfully"*. Clearly there is still work to be done in arguing the case with decision-makers in schools for this kind of investment in their staff.

INSET
"Teachers require ongoing opportunities for training and development, with access to advice, books and writers."
(From Looking Glass to Spyglass)

There is a distinction to be made between writing workshops for teachers, which offer time, space and encouragement for them to enjoy being creative themselves; and INSET focusing on teaching strategies and methods. Teachers need both, and the two approaches can be successfully combined in one experience.

A number of pioneering projects have achieved this, including poetryclass, an initiative run by the Poetry Society, offering training days for teachers led by poets. This is training with a difference, based on the principle that teachers too need creative time, and that those who enjoy writing themselves will teach it well. The enthusiastic response from teachers makes it clear that they agree: an LEA literacy consultant wrote to the Poetry Society that *"many of the teachers said it was the best INSET they had ever attended"*. Alongside the writing, these sessions provide opportunities for teachers to raise and discuss questions and concerns about poetry teaching. The ideas and exercises they try out themselves are translated for use in the classroom, together with ideas for extending, adapting and following them up.

A stand-alone training day for a whole department or staff can breathe new life into the teaching of writing. Included in a residency, it embeds the project in the school and dramatically increases value for money. The project co-ordinator, writer or teacher can take the initiative by suggesting that some time in a residency is set aside for work with teachers. Schools and co-ordinators should expect to pay a higher fee for this service, as they would to any other training provider.

It is important to recognise that delivering INSET requires substantial, up-to-date knowledge of the curriculum, so that the writer can understand the requirements and constraints faced by teachers. 'Training the trainers' is a specialist task, demanding in different ways from classroom work. Writers should not offer it unless they are confident and well-prepared. There is an opportunity here for organisations to lead the way by making high quality training available to experienced writers who want to use their skills in this way.

WRITING WORKSHOP
"When I started teaching I was enthusiastic about writing poems with students, but at the same time, I was uneasy about it. This unease is shared by many English teachers I speak to. It was like trying to show students how to draw and paint, armed only with qualifications in Art History."
Cliff Yates (Jumpstart Poetry in the Secondary School)

The teachers' workshop is not a place for talking about teaching, literacy objectives or how to grade pupils' work. It's time out of a hectic professional life for teachers to concentrate on themselves as creative individuals. It's an oasis, a chance for refreshment and renewal. Teachers gather, perhaps for a couple of hours after school, and take part in a writing workshop designed specially for them. They try out some writing exercises in a safe environment where everyone is in the same boat.

Teachers often begin by saying "I'm not very creative". If this were to be believed, it would be devastating news for our children's futures! But the writer will not take it at face value, recognising instead that the workshop is an unfamiliar experience and can make all first-timers feel vulnerable and wary. Teachers asked to share their work with a group will empathise with students who fear it might not be 'good enough'. Indeed, this is an important function of the teachers' workshop: it's a reminder of how it feels to write under pressure and read out raw new work. We are all self-critical at moments like this. Workshop participants often preface their reading with mutterings – "mine's wrong/rubbish/not very good" – and then proceed to read something brilliant. The writer can reduce anxiety by reassuring teachers that they will not be judged by what they produce. Everything is allowed, and it's more about vision, ideas and enthusiasm than polish and completeness.

Outstanding model projects in this field include one led by Michael Rosen and Myra Barrs (Centre for Language in Primary Education) and documented in the book A Year with Poetry. Over the course of the school year 1994/95, a group of primary teachers met three or four times a term to read, write and talk about poetry. Sometimes the teachers took turns to lead workshops for the others. The book includes chapters written by teachers, describing how they took the experiences back into the classroom and used them to enliven their teaching. Another project, Write Words, offered primary and secondary teachers in Leicestershire a series of workshops with professional writers. The project grew as a partnership between Chris Jones, Literature Officer with Leicestershire County Council, and keen individuals from schools, the Local Education Authority, The Libraries Service and the Arts and Museums Service. Even a one-off workshop for teachers is worthwhile, but extended projects like these have a special value and make a lasting difference. Chris Jones notes that *"as a consequence of the Write Words project... some of the teachers involved have started their own writing groups, and others have actually had their work published"*. What better role model could young writers possibly have than a teacher who is also a published writer?

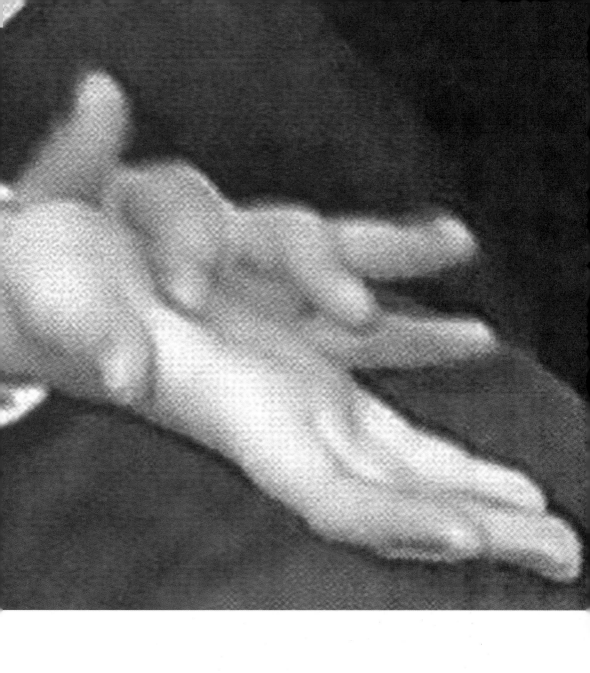

AFTER

Celebrate: an end product

Has the writer's visit been planned with an event or end product in mind? In this section we look at some ways of celebrating a successful project.

Live Literature: Performance

"Children and young people perform poems all the time, whether they know it or not: rhymes, raps, dips, gags, jokes, songs, chants, lists, knockabouts, flitting in and out of everyday life, and it's the job of the poet to capture the words and help them to fly, and to help the children and young people make them fly."
Ian McMillan (Reading the Applause)

Young people – even shy ones – amaze their teachers with the enthusiasm they bring to a performance. It is a chance to gain peer recognition, and to experience first-hand the interplay between audience and writer/performer. As Philip Pullman says: *"the audience in the dark are makers, too"* (Times Educational Supplement). If a performance is planned at the outset, work can be written to reflect a range of styles, multiple voices, and variety in tone, rhythm and pacing. Build in rehearsal time at the start.

"One of the best moments was seeing their faces split into big grins as they got up to read at the sharing day."
Kevin McCann (Times Educational Supplement)

An obvious venue is the school hall, with the school community or a wider, invited audience. Smaller, more intimate events are perfect for the school library. Work can be taken on a 'tour' round all the other classes in the school; in fact, a whole project can be designed around older students writing for younger audiences.

Young writers will usually want to read their own work, but there is a difference between reading and performing, and some may prefer to delegate. Hearing someone else read your work aloud can be enlightening and validating.

Publicity lets the wider community see what your school has achieved. Local radio may be interested in using extracts of recordings, and local newspapers or regional TV arts programmes may feature your project.

The Art of Words: Display

We are all familiar with the wall of handwritten poems mounted on sugar paper – it's a strong favourite in schools. But access to computers opens up many exciting ways of displaying text. Short poems can be enlarged to one word a page and used on a much more dramatic scale. Texts such as plays or stories don't have to be exempt because of their length; an excerpt of dialogue, accompanied by illustrations of characters or ideas for set design, can look stunning. The project may already have been recorded through interviews, photographs or video, and the display can include this documentation.

Poems look beautiful on tracing paper or acetate and coloured to look like stained-glass-window text. Working with artists and writers, young people can display work in a more permanent way using mosaic or sculpture to be placed in the school grounds or specific sites in the area. One example of text in public art is Stonepoems, a celebration of the town of Halewood where the Windows Project and Halewood Arts Association worked with an artist to incorporate children's poems into sculptures in the local park and railway station.

The Power of Print: Publication
"Seeing their work in print can give an enormous boost to children's self-esteem and having their poems in an anthology or up on the classroom wall can have a huge effect on their motivation towards literature."
Valerie Bloom (The Poetry Book for Primary Schools)

Print is the lifeblood of literature. Publishing is an adventure which expands the students' experience: from initial idea to watching someone read text with your name at the end of it! Each job teaches valuable skills – editing, design, illustration, book-making, marketing – and can be tackled as teamwork. The end result can be as simple as one-off origami books, or as spectacular as a giant scrapbook or residency diary. A 3D element is possible with mini-books and zigzag folded books. Paul Johnson has written a number of publications on the subject; see more at www.btinternet.com/~bookart.

As Michael Rosen says: *"Classrooms could be mini-publishing houses... Children can become expert on what makes books attractive and interesting. Their books can sit alongside the best of children's literature and be read and reread many, many times"* (Did I Hear You Write?).

When thinking of print, don't be confined to books. Simple publications like bookmarks can be designed on the computer, photocopied onto coloured card and cut to size in one afternoon. They cost only a few pence a dozen to make, and can be distributed to the public library, parents and students. By reducing a short poem on the photocopier it is possible to create tiny poems by students. All letters from the school should have a poem in the corner.

Budgeted for and done well, a more serious publication can have a huge impact on the school and wider community, and assist in attracting funding for future projects. Some schools share costs and create a book with contributions from one year-group each. Here are a few planning considerations to make your book a success:

Publication: a checklist

- Plan more than one contact session to generate the writing; build in editing and redrafting time with the teacher. Without time to develop, first drafts to an initial writing exercise will have a 'sameness' and contain obvious mistakes.

- Call a printer for quotes. The book will probably either be stapled (up to 30 printed pages), or perfect-bound. 64 printed pages are usually enough. Take a look at books in the school library to help decide size and length.

- Budget for a typesetter and/or designer. If the writer is to do it, an additional fee will be needed.

- Allow time for pupils to produce black and white illustrations.

- Clearly mark each piece of work with the pupil's name, school and year group. If for any reason the school cannot get permission from parents, use initials instead.

- If the writer is producing the book, the school or co-ordinator should help with proof-reading and negotiating with the printer. It's a big responsibility for one person to get right!

- An ISBN number makes it seem like' a 'proper' book, but unless it is to be sold through orders in book shops it may not be worth the expense. You can achieve properness in other ways, such as designing your own imprint (or publisher's name) and holding a book launch with bottles of pop and a big bunch of flowers for the book team. This could not be more appropriate, since the word 'anthology' is from the Greek, meaning *a bouquet of flowers*.

Writer and editor Graham Denton gives the following advice on selecting work for an anthology: *"I think the best anthologies are undoubtedly those perfectly weighted and balanced with just the right combinations of poems. They read as a whole; not as a collection of individual scraps scattered randomly throughout the book with no connection, but as carefully chosen pieces, each making a connection with the next, so that the book, like a good story, has a beginning, middle and an end"*.

What next?

You've only just waved the writer off and you're already feeling that sense of anticlimax. Is it all over?

Certainly not! Don't let the excitement and the learning drain away. View the writer's time with you as the start of a new creative writing culture in your school. There's plenty you can do to keep the momentum going.

Follow-up resources

If the value of the writer's visit is to be maximised, the teacher should think early on about what he or she might need in order to follow up the work effectively. Enlist the writer's help with this. Many writers will be happy to provide copies of exercises or have their brains picked for other resources such as books, websites and competitions.

Get connected

There is plenty of information and support out there: see *Organisations* and *Websites*. Taking out schools membership with the Poetry Society, NAWE, the Poetry Book Society and others will entitle you and your pupils to all sorts of resources and make you feel 'part of the action'.

Continuing contact

With prior negotiation, writers are often delighted to be sent copies of finished pieces. Don't overlook the traditional 'letter to the author' – a chance for young readers to respond to the writer's own work. Alan Garner says that at their best these letters *"break down the necessary isolation of the writer and create a sense of community: not community of flattery, but a community of caring, emotion and of vision shared"* (The Voice that Thunders).

More ambitiously, a project is sometimes planned to create a long-term relationship between school and writer. This can continue to thrive for years, with successive year-groups of pupils looking forward to their turn to work with 'our writer'.

Competitions

Entering a creative writing competition can be very motivating; even the simple discipline of a deadline is a useful focus. Be aware, though, that some competitions are more reputable than others. Unscrupulous publishers sometimes mail schools, advertising 'competitions', then going on to cram all the entries into an anthology which they sell aggressively at a high price. Those dealing in this sharp practice know that proud parents and grandparents will buy.

Ask your writer to help you identify worthwhile opportunities, and use this checklist as a rule of thumb:

- students should not have to pay to enter;
- contributors to an anthology should receive at least one free copy;
- copyright should remain with the writer.

Remind students that competition judges always wish for more prizes to give out, and that if you are not a winner this does not mean your writing is inferior.

Getting published

Kate Jones, editor of Young Writer magazine, says: "I'm always on the lookout for new young writers to publish in the next issue". Details of this and other websites and magazines which publish young people's work can be found at the back of this book.

Writers' notebooks

Giving each pupil a private notebook is a very significant thing to do. It encourages them to work in the way 'real' writers work. Tell them to use the notebook for all the thoughts, ideas, notes and jottings that might one day make useful material for stories and poems. From time to time you might like to suggest (but not insist on) a specific task: watch an animal or bird, and make notes on its behaviour; watch someone carrying out an ordinary domestic task, like washing-up; look around a familiar room and find a detail you think no one has ever noticed before. Resist the temptation to give too many instructions, and remember: in order to experiment safely, writers need to know that their notebooks are *genuinely* private.

Assemblies

Reading out in assembly is a common way of celebrating a writing project, and there's no reason why it should stop there. Pupils' writing can be made a regular feature of assemblies and other gatherings. With practice, pupils will gain confidence and performance skills.

Writers' group

Capitalise on the rush of enthusiasm created by the writer's visit by setting up a lunchtime writers' group for pupils. There are many thriving examples in primary and secondary schools, led by keen teachers and perhaps the occasional visiting writer. The writers' group is workshop-based and young people find it quite a different experience from English lessons. Everyone is on an equal footing; they learn to experiment, play with ideas and language, and give and receive positive criticism. Once the group is established, there is no reason why participants themselves should not take turns to plan and lead exercises. And when one or two colleagues start to show an interest, think about starting an after-school version for staff…

Reading group

Capitalise on the current popularity of reading groups by offering one in your school library. Following up a writer's visit in this way emphasises to pupils that reading and writing are two sides of the same coin. One school librarian told us of a project in her school: *"We asked members of staff to select their favourite books and then create a calendar. For each month there is a photograph of the member of staff plus the reason for their choice"*. Try doing the same with pupils' choices. Reading groups can also write and display their reviews and are the perfect host for 'book-exchange' projects where pupils swap books they've read.

A recent research project brought US-style 'literature circles' to South Lanarkshire schools; these operate like reading groups but meet during class time. Flora Kennedy, one of the teachers involved, said: *"Reading, writing, talking and listening: I am able to get all these facets of language into the one lesson"* (Times Educational Supplement).

Residential courses

For a genuinely life-changing experience, take your students on a residential course. These are offered by several organisations, including the Arvon Foundation and the Taliesin Trust. Both run courses for young people aged 10 - 18 at their various centres in England, Scotland and Wales. The group lives and works with two professional writers, in an atmosphere where everyone is treated as a writer. Teachers who have taken the plunge almost invariably speak of the dramatic impact these courses have had on their students' writing, and on their wider lives: *"It was such a rewarding experience. The students' confidence and written work improved and developed a real maturity."*

The students themselves also have high praise for the courses: *"[The course tutors] were amazing – they were so kind and taught us so much – I will take this experience with me for the rest of my life"*.

These are highly enjoyable professional development experiences for teachers, and once bitten by the bug schools tend to return year after year with new groups of students. Arvon and the Taliesin Trust are committed to the principle of access for all, and financial assistance is available to schools which need it. Find out more at: www.arvonfoundation.org or www.tynewydd.org

Teachers with a personal interest in writing should also consider signing up for a course in their own right. Open courses, available to all adults, take place throughout the year and offer the opportunity to learn amongst like-minded people. Both organisations produce brochures with details of their open programmes, and Arvon offers special bursaries to practising teachers.

Writers: keeping the balance

For the writer working with schools, nearly every day is the first day at work. Each journey is an unknown; each workplace, car park, timetable and group of students is new. To make no bones about it: this work can be exhausting. For all but the most outgoing, the emotional output is comparable to a solo theatre show. Even during lunch the writer keeps up a public face, responding appropriately to comments on how lovely it must be to travel, sign books and ponder the muse.

But this is common to all freelance artists, and we persevere because the work is intensely rewarding. It allows writers to develop their skills and passions and share the buzz of creative energy with young people. Later we will look in more detail at these rewards. For some writers, schools work is just one item in a portfolio of part-time and short-term jobs: tutoring residential courses, judging competitions, editing anthologies, programming festivals or managing projects on behalf of other writers. Whatever the individual circumstances, it provides a welcome source of income for the writer. This chapter explores ways of managing the financial, practical and other implications.

WHY DO WRITERS WORK IN SCHOOLS?

"One of the main reasons I grew up was so that I wouldn't have to go to school. But I sometimes visit schools if they're interested in making magic – I mean poetry."
Adrian Mitchell (There's a poet behind you)

It's not for the fame and adulation that writers start going into schools, though it can have its moments; Paul Cookson relates how *"a kid in Doncaster once asked for my autograph and then said 'Thanks. I'll put that up on my wall next to my picture of Fred Dibnah'"* (www.poetryzone.co.uk).

For children's writers, it can be an obvious step. As Alan Gibbons says: *"The children are the audience, the book-buyers (or, at least, the people who persuade the book-buyers to part with their money). In short, they are the air the writer breathes"* (Writing in Education). Publishers receive many requests from teachers, and see the author visit as a good way of promoting books and raising the author's profile, not only with children but also with teachers, school librarians and parents. More generally, spending time with young people is a real opportunity to influence the way they think about literature, both as creators and as consumers. When we go into schools we play a part in developing the readers and writers of tomorrow.

Money is another important factor. Teachers do not always understand the economics of 'being a writer'. There are notable exceptions, but most writers survive on a modest income, and working in schools offers a way for them to earn from their skills and experience. One reason why there are so many more poets in schools than novelists or journalists is that poets – even the ones with dozens of books and awards behind them – cannot make a living out of writing and publishing alone. Schools projects are one way of supporting and enabling the writer's own creative work.

A writer just starting to consider schools work might do the maths and get quite excited at the prospect of earning £250 a day. But realism sets in very quickly. One day's work in a school equals at least two days when you factor in the planning and preparation, and the time spent developing your infrastructure (reading, research, creating new workshop exercises, taking part in training and professional development). And that's before you even start to consider the time you need for your own writing.

Anyway, working in schools is so demanding that no writer would be likely to continue doing it for long unless they enjoyed it and felt it was important. At heart, most writers who work in schools are deeply committed to the value of creative work with young people. As David Morley puts it, *"idealism draws writers into the classroom"*. When writers talked to us about the pleasures of education work, they nearly all enthused about the same things: watching young people grow, develop, become enthusiastic and absorbed themselves:

"The look of pleasure, joy and realisation on the face of a young writer when they are working on a piece and find some treasure, or when they are reading out work and enjoying it and proud of it."

"Days when the formal classroom dissolves away, because the whole group is enthusiastically engaged... it becomes a group of eager, self-motivated, curious, exploring writers."

"Meeting new kids, sharing their enthusiasm for writing and books, watching their confidence grow, seeing their delight in what they have made."

HOW DOES IT AFFECT THE WRITER'S OWN WORK?

For some, there is an absolute division between their writing and their facilitating lives, a division they describe as *"essential"* and *"a form of self-protection"*. We have already highlighted the problems writers can face if they become swamped by education work to the extent where it threatens to exhaust and deplete them.

For others, though – perhaps those who have managed to achieve a comfortable balance – there is a reciprocal relationship between the two. The American organisation Teachers & Writers Collaborative published an interesting book on this subject: The Point: Where Teaching and Writing Intersect. In it a group of writers articulate what they have learned from their work with students:

"Teaching writing forced me to analyse my own writing process, and I eventually came away with an understanding of it that led to better writing for me."

"It helps me from spiralling off into some mental ivory tower, keeps me in touch with my original feelings about poetry."

"I feel a little sorry for poets who don't teach writing... my students have forced me to extend myself by demanding authenticity of feeling and experience. They have brought me closer to reality simply by being there. No one can go consistently into the classroom and remain unchanged."

TIME

Being successfully self-employed depends on your ability to cost and manage time accurately. As well as contact hours, the writer must also figure in time for planning, preparation, follow-up and administration. Travel and overnight stays can extend a four-hour contact job to two days. If you take a writer's daily rate and multiply it by five, you will not arrive at a weekly wage because *each job takes at least twice as long* as the hours actually paid for.

We need better terms to differentiate between a writer's own writing time and paid facilitation projects such as work in schools. For the purposes of this book, we define them as *craft time* and *contact time,* and keeping the two balanced requires all the skill of a juggler. This feeling of imbalance is not just about hours in a day, but also about energy, focus and professional development. It may seem possible to get writing done in the 'blank' days in the diary, but without the commitment to defend them those days will be swallowed.

Contact time is an immediate source of income, and comes with an outside structure and a deadline. When bookings clamour so authoritatively for attention, writing, researching and redrafting get left at the bottom of the pile. Sadly it is almost unheard of for a writing commission to be part of a residency in primary or secondary education and so the challenge for writers is to be practising artists within a structure that rewards their enabling skills and not their art.

Writers' work in schools must not cut them off from their writing. It's our intense connection with the art itself that guides us when teaching its techniques and it's the excellence of the art that defines the success of a project. Teachers can share skill and passion too; what is the extra ingredient that writers bring to the classroom? *The very fact that they are practising writers.*

KEEPING YOUR WRITING A PRIORITY
"There's a new profession – writers in schools. Some are good writers and produce great work with the children… yet some of them might be so driven to help others that they lose sight of their own writing, and become a kind of professional automaton, a hermit crab shell of a writer."
David Morley (Writing in Education)

It is easy to get into the habit of dividing your time between 'paid work' (schools or other contact projects) and 'unpaid work' (own writing). This is a mistake. Your writing career is a long-term investment. If it is neglected, the writer who happens to work in schools can morph into a writer who *only* works in schools. There are bursaries and grants offered by Arts Councils and literature organisations to help you 'buy back' time to write. Fellowships and retreats also offer ways of supporting writing and research time (see *Organisations* and *Websites*).

TRAINING AND PROFESSIONAL DEVELOPMENT FOR WRITERS
When we asked writers whether they would welcome training in good practice and the creative possibilities of working in schools, an overwhelming majority said yes. They listed a variety of specific training needs, from "working in multimedia" to "working with other artforms" and "the national curriculum". Even widely published children's authors are often asked by their publishers to undergo professional training in order to work with young people.

Training… me?
A handful of the writers we asked were resistant to the idea of training or professional development in any form. This seems curious, since training is a feature of almost everyone's working life, from judges to bus drivers.

The positive side of lone working is that it allows the individual writer a great deal of autonomy and control in every stage of the work. Those who succeed are likely to be 'self-starters' who value their independence and self-reliance. It's unfortunate, however, if this stops acknowledging that we have things to learn from each other. As one writer said, *"none of us knows all the answers"*.

Initial training
The need for training is most acute among writers just starting out on schools work. This kind of training is now offered by a number of organisations, and there is one central resource providing information on all training opportunities in the field: www.literaturetraining.com

The ingredients vary from one programme to another. Titles of recent training sessions run by NAWE include Developing Your Career as a Freelance Writer in

85

Education; A Good Toolkit – Workshop Skills for Primary and Secondary Schools; and An Update on The National Curriculum for Writers. The first two were led by practising writers with long experience of schools work, and the third by an LEA Literacy Consultant. In Scotland, Live Literature Scotland runs a programme of professional development opportunities, Words@Work, which includes sessions on schools work.

Any initial training programme needs to contain some basic information on current policy and practice in schools: most writers, like other adults, will not have spent time in school since they were pupils themselves (back in the Dark Ages, or the Golden Age, depending on your perspective!). They may have little idea about the momentous changes that have taken place over the past 15 years.

Apprenticeship

A programme of training sessions can be combined with mentoring or shadowing opportunities. Nothing prepares the beginner for schools work as effectively as observing and assisting a more experienced writer in the classroom. Approaches and styles of working vary so much that ideally there should be chances to shadow two or three different writers. A gradual shift from observing to leading a session allows the shadower to experiment within a 'safe' environment. Comments from the Northern Artists into Schools Mentoring Project reveal the impact this sort of training had on writers:

"It generally gave me more confidence to interact in a classroom situation."

"I was able to see how someone else organises a project, works in the classroom, plans beforehand etc. It was reassuring for me and I learnt some good tips and approaches."

Mentoring involves a sustained commitment over weeks or even months. The mentor offers support, encouragement and advice in a series of meetings or phone calls. It requires skill on the part of the project co-ordinator in matching two compatible writers, and a clear structure to keep learning focused and relevant.

We have heard of organisations which employ writers on a 'trainee' or 'probationary' basis, and pay lower fees accordingly. Writers agreeing to this should make sure that the terms of the arrangement are clear: when does the probationary period end, and how will you know that you have 'passed'? In return for accepting a lower rate, you should feel able to request a varied programme of work experience, and ask for support as required during this phase.

86

Continuous professional development

As writers in education, we have a continuing need for support throughout our careers. We need training in new technology (how many writers are confident users of the interactive whiteboard?) and we need to keep refreshing our knowledge and skills in response to a changing curriculum. In other professions, opportunities like these would be available as a matter of course, throughout every stage of a career, to freelancers as well as employees. We see no reason why they should not be available to writers.

There is demand amongst even the most experienced writers for professional development, sharing and networking opportunities. There are many advantages in getting experienced writers together to pool experiences and learn from one another. Each writer is a treasure-house of ideas and methods; while a few of these might qualify as 'trade secrets', others can be shared, modified and adapted to broaden and enrich the work of others.

The recurring request – and it is so prevalent and so strongly worded that it amounts to a *longing* – is for opportunities to meet other writers and share experiences:

"Even though my diary is full for 12 months or more, I have no idea what others in the field charge for their work, how they organise their visits and what activities they offer. It would be great to have some sort of forum..."

"I would give my left arm for the chance to observe a few other writers in action in the classroom – seeing alternative approaches would keep me from getting stuck in a rut."

"I would really value peer support groups of experienced writers, preferably with a wide range of different experience, age focus, etc... the best learning I've had from other people has been by analogy, I think – making connections – rather than being instructed."

"Days simply sharing workshop ideas are really useful and inspiring."

But what kind of provision would be useful? It is relatively easy to imagine a basic 'toolkit' of skills and knowledge for writers at the start of their careers in schools, but the needs of more experienced practitioners are less well identified.

One model we know well is the preparation for the poetryclass INSET project. Planning days were held for the poets who were to deliver the training to teachers. They came together in groups of 8 – 12, to discuss the philosophy behind the project and to work out how the training would be structured and delivered. Each poet was also asked to bring along one tried-and-tested writing

87

exercise and run it with the group. Finally, an LEA adviser was invited to give some background information on the curriculum and the Literacy Strategy – a session which invariably gave rise to lively and important debate.

The cost of these planning days was met from the poetryclass budget, yet their value extended way beyond the boundaries of this one project, throughout the poets' work in classrooms and staff-rooms up and down the land. There is surely a case for funding to be made available to allow more of this kind of sharing, discussion and peer-group learning between experienced writers.

Funding

There are financial issues involved in offering professional development to writers: as freelancers they do not find it easy to meet the costs and earmark unpaid days. Like all projects, successful training requires proper funding as well as inspiration. There are often bursaries and subsidies available to help writers take part; find out more about these at www.literaturetraining.com.

As one writer puts it: *"One can always benefit from further training if it is relevant and well delivered. But I have to weigh this against the time at my disposal, the need to survive"*. A number of training and networking initiatives have foundered on the question of finances; either not enough people sign up, or the room is full of aspiring writers – all the experienced practitioners are out there, busy practising!

FREELANCING

Registering as self-employed

Self-employed people must be registered with the Inland Revenue, and must keep books recording income and expenditure, with the receipts to prove it. You will be able to claim some expenses prior to your start-up date; you can get information on this from the Inland Revenue or your local business start-up organisation.

Contracts

A sample contract can be found at www.scottishbooktrust.com. Alternatively, a letter confirming when, where, who and what can act as an informal contract and is invaluable as reference. Do not assume that signing contracts is merely a formality. It is advisable to read them carefully, as they may include details that you were not expecting. We have heard of cases where contracts include intellectual copyright clauses, requiring writers to sign over rights to any work produced during the residency. This is unusual, and we advise writers not to sign such contracts without seeking advice on the copyright implications and negotiating proper commission fees.

Invoicing

Schools will expect a writer to be self-employed, and many local authorities will require a tax code or National Insurance number before you can be paid. A clearly laid out invoice is essential. Make a duplicate copy for your own records. Invoices can be presented before you leave if you have prior agreement with the school to be paid on the day. If payment is not received within a month, a duplicate copy on red paper with 'Monthly Invoice Reminder' across the top can do the trick.

Tax

When taking an overview of uneven annual earnings, remember that a portion of your income must be set aside in readiness for your tax bill. After your individual tax allowance (which varies depending on your circumstances) you will be liable for tax and National Insurance which can amount to 28% or more of your earnings. An accountant used to dealing with artists and writers can explain exactly the full range of items which count as 'allowable expenses'; an initial consultation can be a worthwhile (and tax-deductible) investment.

Deductibles

If you work from home there will be deductible expenses (a fraction of your heating, light, rent and other bills). For more information on tax reliefs and deductibles, check the annually updated Writers' & Artists' Yearbook, or The Writer's Handbook . Make it a rule to keep receipts, and when paying in cheques make a note of what proportion is pay (taxable) and what proportion is expenses (deductible).

Publicity

Many writers nowadays have their own (or collective) websites. This is a valuable way of letting the world see samples of your writing, your photo, your work experience and rates. Being included on an organisation's website is also worthwhile. However, if this is your only publicity, you may be seen as working exclusively in association with that one organisation, rather than being a freelancer who can be approached independently.

A surprising amount of a writer's life is taken up by things other than writing! But we are a resilient lot, and will find ways to keep writing central to our lives even if it means we do most of it on boats, trains and aeroplanes!

"I write around 1000 words each day when I'm at home. If I'm going out all day to talk in schools or libraries then I scribble 500 words on the journey."
Jacqueline Wilson (Young Writer)

Languages

Traddodiad a naddodd y graig   *Tradition shaped the rock*
A'r iaith wedi nydda'r pridd   *And the language spun the soil*
Llygaid y barcud sy'n gwylo   *The eyes of the kite watching*
A chwmni hen ffrind yw'r ffridd.   *The mountain pasture is like an old friend.*

extract from the poem 'Cwm Croes' by Mared Griffiths (12)
(A Special Place: poems by the members of Gwynedd Writing Squads)

This section is about language, and just as crucially it is about a sense of place and belonging. The study of etymology, like archaeology, reveals the history of new cultures emerging while others battle against extinction. The writer Iwan Llwyd says in his introduction to this anthology, produced by young people attending writing weekends at Tŷ Newydd in North Wales: *"In the celebrity world of the global village, people sometimes forget the depth and richness of the local and the traditional. In North Wales we are lucky enough to live in a part of the world where the language, culture and traditions have a memory of at least 2,000 years. Some of the secrets of those long lost times are still alive in the place names all around us, the names of farms and rivers, mountains and valleys, islands and fields".*

This deep need to respect tradition and collective memory will be recognised by communities throughout Britain. Arts Council Northern Ireland says that *"Irish and Ulster-Scots language arts are living elements of Northern Ireland's cultural heritage",* and in Scotland a number of projects are dedicated to keeping marginalised languages alive and strong.

There are over 300 languages spoken in Britain today. For young people, using another language or exploring their mother-tongue is fundamental to their sense of self and their growth as writers. Visiting authors play a vital role in this development, because language is their passion and this passion is infectious. That's why writers value the power of language – its cadences, its bluntness, its secrets. Whether it's Iwan Llwyd on Welsh, Debjani Chatterjee on Urdu or Matthew Fitt on Scots, this passion shines through.

We don't see books like this
Debjani Chatterjee

"It did not take me long to finish reading the book (Grandma's Treasure Trove / Dadimar Jhapi by Rashida Islam). I have read it more than once. Every page has Bengali and English. We don't see books like this in my school. Bengali is my mother tongue. Next summer our mum will take Shahzad and me to Bangladesh for two months so that we can learn Bengali. Maybe I will then be able to read the stories in Bengali. I am learning French at school. I can sing a French song. It begins: Bonjour! Bonsoir! Some children can learn Spanish. But nobody can learn Bengali in my school."

Educational psychologists agree that it is important for children to enjoy a good grounding in their mother tongue. Among other things this can actually help them in learning a second language. Nevertheless, the experience of many children who have another language is rather discouraging in British schools; the mother tongue is often totally ignored or otherwise devalued. So a linguistic dichotomy can develop between their lives at home and at school. Children may learn to speak their mother tongue at home, but will generally be illiterate in that language unless the parents either make a special effort to teach it themselves or send the children to a weekly 'community language school' or – as sometimes happens in the case of South Asian immigrants – take them for an 'immersion' holiday in the Indian sub-continent.

I met eight-year-old Feryal Khan through a community group in Sheffield and gave her a book by Rashida Islam to review for the magazine, *Writing in Education*. But what a valuable message of endorsement she would have received if the bilingual book had been a 'school' book and the review had been a school exercise. Like most schools in England, hers offered a European second language but neglected South Asian languages that are her city's second, third and fourth languages. This means that when I, as a writer, translator or storyteller, visit a school, I am sometimes conscious of an added role that I may need to fulfil – that of an ambassador for my languages and the cultures that they carry.

This was the case, for instance, just last week when I visited Wednesbury as part of an imaginative 'Adopt an Author' project, run by Sampad, a Birmingham-based South Asian arts organisation. Over several weeks Year 5 children had read one of my poetry books, *Animal Antics*, and exchanged correspondence with me by e-mail. Then came the face-to-face encounter over a buffet lunch with the children. Nearly a third of the class had a South Asian background and most of these were British Bangladeshis with a Sylheti dialect of Bengali as their mother tongue, but there were also one or two with Punjabi and Hindi. They looked at the display of my books for young readers and the bilingual children among them were especially excited to see a few bilingual books, even though only two children were actually able to read the Bengali titles. During our lunch I had quite a few children come up to me, individually, to request that I 'say something' in Bengali and Hindi. This was easily done, but I think that what will have benefited the class as a whole was listening to a Bengali poem by Rabindranath Tagore, along with my translation, and an invitation to try out tongue-twisters in South Asian languages during the afternoon performance.

A simple thing like a Punjabi Sikh child recognising a Punjabi Sikh greeting in a story or a poem can give that child an empowering experience at the same time that it offers all the children an authentic flavour of multi-cultural and multi-lingual Britain. If a writer has other languages, I would definitely recommend that they try using them in their work with children. I would love to see every school in Britain celebrating World Mother Language Day (21st February), and an excellent way of doing so might be to invite writers and artists to contribute to a multilingual performance of poetry and songs. And children will respond well to the monolingual writer who is clearly enthusiastic about their languages and respects them enough to have made the effort to learn at least a little.

The literatures and literary forms that other languages offer are also a valuable resource for any writer, and many teachers are appreciative of writers and translators introducing students to such riches as the ghazal in Urdu and Hindi, the pantoum in Malay, the ai-nitam in Assamese and the haiku in Japanese. Firstly there are the poems by great exponents of the forms in their original languages. So students will benefit from reading – and hearing – the ghazals of such masters as Mirza Ghalib (1797-1869) and Nasir Kazmi (1925-1972), and the haiku of such masters as Basho (1644-1694) and Masaoka Shiki (1867-1902), in both Urdu and Japanese and of course in translation. They will benefit too from experiencing the contemporary ghazals and haiku written in English by the writer visiting their school. This will bring home to them the fact that the ghazal, the haiku and other verse forms have already found a home in English poetry, and will give them some awareness of how these forms are being adapted in the process. Of course the writer can also explain how a poetic form like the sonnet has also journeyed from its Italian origin to become a mainstay of English literature.

Debjani Chatterjee was born in India and grew up in many Asian and African countries. She has written, edited and translated many books of prose and poetry for children and adults, most recently *Namaskar: New and Selected Poems and Masala*. Debjani chairs the National Association of Writers in Education and runs Sahitya Press. Sheffield Hallam University awarded her an honorary doctorate in 2002.

Scots language in schools   *Matthew Fitt*

Many children in Scotland are bilingual in both the English and the Scots languages. For a long time now....

Hang on: Scots? A language? Bilingual? Some of you may be struggling with the reference to bilingualism, others thinking it odd, even ridiculous to apply the term 'language' to something called 'Scots'.

You'll be in for a surprise then to learn that Scots is now recognised as a language by the EU, the UK Government, the Scottish Executive and that the General Records Office of Scotland puts the number of Scots speakers at 1.6 million.

And if you reckon that Scots is Gaelic, reckon again. Scots is a Germanic language closely related to English, in the same way that Norwegian is to Danish, Czech to Slovak and Spanish to Catalan.

Here are a few Scots words to keep you going – *ken, hoose, coo, greetin, mingin, bonnie, drookit, crabbit, gutties, breeks* and *scunner*. These are just a sample of the rich vocabulary many Scottish children bring to school.

And here, with its wheel stuck in the ditch, is the problem.

Scots might be the language with their family and peers but when a Scots speaking pupil enters the classroom, he or she is expected to switch to English. For the past two hundred years it has been the aim of Scottish educators to develop their pupils skills in English – and there is of course nothing wrong with this. Equipping young Scots with the ability to use the world's lingua franca is an essential role of Scottish education. But at what cost to those children whose home language is Scots?

In school, when pupils are engaging formally with language, they do so through English. When being encouraged to read, the texts offered will almost invariably be in English.

What if a child lacks confidence in English? What if they feel more comfortable using Scots? What is the provision for such pupils? Sadly, very little. Once a year reciting poems by Burns or other writers, Scots speaking children are given the chance to express themselves in the classroom in their own language. Next day, it's back to English.

In the absence of any serious provision for Scots speakers in an English-only learning environment, visits to schools by writers who speak and write in Scots are extremely valuable. A Scots poet in a classroom is like a bull in the proverbial china shop, breaking all the linguistic rules. Children hear someone using Scots in the class and not being told off. They witness an adult talking a different language from all other adults (except maybe the janitor and kitchen staff) in the school. And they are experiencing possibly for the first time someone talking in Scots about serious issues, about the big stories of life and death.

And starved of their own culture in schools, Scots speaking pupils simply love visits from Scots writers. Boys in particular who are reluctant normally to pick up a book will demand to read more in Scots. Children teachers have identified as quiet or shy will suddenly come to life when Scots is read to them.

While the Scottish education system continues to ignore the benefits to Scots speaking pupils of integrating the Scots Language into their study, it is crucial that Scots writers like Christine de Luca, James Robertson, Hamish MacDonald, Sheena Blackhall, Janet Paisley and Liz Lochhead be invited to read to thousands of children each year.

Matthew Fitt is Schools Officer for the Scottish Arts Council project, Itchy Coo
www.itchy-coo.com

News from elsewhere

This is not an attempt to look at the 'whole picture', but a few glimpses into how schools and writers work together in other parts of the world. In some countries there is a thriving tradition of writers-in-schools work; in others it's a new idea which has not yet taken root. Looking beyond our national borders, we can see that there are experiences we in Britain can learn from, and also opportunities for us to share our experience with others just starting out.

Ireland
Poetry Ireland, the national organisation for poetry in Ireland, runs a highly structured Writers In Schools Scheme offering part-funded visits by writers of all kinds (not just poets) to primary and secondary schools. Each school can apply for either an A type or a B type visit: A type is 120 - 150 minutes and B type is 300 minutes. The B visit can, if schools wish, take place over a maximum period of two weeks, divided into no more than five one-hour sessions. More recently the Scheme has developed to include longer residencies, in which the writer works with one single class and teacher throughout. Poetry Ireland Education describes the thinking behind these residencies: *"To take a more developmental approach towards the teaching of literature and to develop approaches, which enable the participants to explore the world of the imagination over a longer period of time, in the company of an experienced writer. The participation of a key teacher and the development of a working alliance between the teacher and writer is fundamental to this approach"*.

All writers involved in the Scheme have at least one book published by a publisher with national distribution, or one work staged by a theatre company funded by the Arts Council. Some writers work in the Irish language as well as in English. Details of writers are available on the Poetry Ireland website.

Poetry Ireland also organises In-service Programmes for teachers at both Primary and Secondary level, delivered by working writers in conjunction with the various Teacher Education Centres around the country, and occasional seminars for writers on best practice in the classroom.

Europe
The European Network on Poetry and Education is a new venture, pioneered by Professor Gloria Bordons at the University of Barcelona. A three-day conference was held in Barcelona in 2004, with contributions from many European countries, including Spain, Italy, France, Slovenia, Ireland, Portugal and Britain. The Network is in its infancy, but already it has put writers, educators and small organisations in touch with one another and created opportunities for them to

95

share information and good practice. As a result it is becoming apparent that there are huge differences in the way writers and schools interact. Franz Andres Morrissey, writer and lecturer at the University of Bern in Switzerland, has observed some of this variety in the course of his career:

"In Switzerland, apparently in Slovakia and (according to some very informal research) in most other European countries, there is a kind of 'museum approach' to writers, with a look-but-don't-touch attitude towards those few writers who stray into schools. Many European countries seem to have a deep-seated doubt that writing can be learnt at all. Writers haven't had to learn; they are gifted, kissed by the muse. It is perhaps this attitude of the literary genius as something 'given' that may explain why, in contrast to mother-tongue teachers, many EFL (English as a Foreign Language) teachers embrace creative writing so much more readily. Furthermore, as EFL has a reputation for leading the field of language methodology, there is a tendency to see creative writing not so much as a literary activity but first and foremost as an innovative language practice.

It would be unfair to say that no Swiss writers are engaged in education. Novelist Emil Zopfi – together with his wife Christa, who describes herself as a Friedenspädagogin, a peace pedagogue, not a writer – have at least two writing workbooks to their name, both in German, both aimed at writers as well as at teachers and students. But it would be an exaggeration to suggest that such writers in education are anything other than rare birds.

By contrast, writing groups and workshops by mainly Anglophone expats, and in some cases published writers, are fairly widespread. With the support of the British Council, well-known poets have conducted workshops in English in Swiss gymnasia (grammar schools), most notably Roger McGough, Benjamin Zephaniah and Ian McMillan.

A similar picture exists, I have found, in Slovakia. A 1999 British Council teachers and writers conference in Budmerice brought together Central and Eastern European writers and teachers from various institutions of secondary and tertiary education with British writers, including Paul Munden, the director of the National Association of Writers in Education. The NAWE model met with considerable interest at the time, but it seems that the only real spin-off to date is a regular summer school in the Tatra Mountains near Budmerice, which brings together Slovak EFL teachers and writers from Britain to explore creative writing techniques and help teachers to develop ideas about its uses in EFL teaching.

It is fair to say that the Anglo-Saxon world – in particular the States and Britain – are ahead of the game in bringing together writers and schools. To name only a few, the New York-based Teachers & Writers Collaborative, NAWE, the Poetry

Society and more recently the British Council have been and are doing sterling work in this respect. I hope that an initiative to set up national networks with the expertise of these official bodies, and encouraging local writers to consider work in schools, may be a first step towards ensuring that future generations of schoolchildren will not only have had the opportunity to write poems, stories and even dramatic sketches in the course of their schooling, but will be able to do so with real-to-the-touch writers in classrooms, instead of hearing them from some distant rostrum."

USA

The USA has a wealth of creative writing activities in communities and in education. Anyone who surfs the net will find many internet-based resources for writers and teachers. As in Britain, some of this writers-in-schools work is promoted and supported by the Poet Laureate. Billy Collins gives this summary of his time in the post: *"The US laureateship has been used as a platform from which to launch national poetry programmes. My programme, called Poetry 180 for the 180 days of the school year, is aimed at getting poetry in the high schools – without having to hold students by the back of the neck while covering scansion"* (Teachers & Writers magazine).

Teachers & Writers Collaborative
The Teachers & Writers Collaborative, based in New York, was founded in 1967 by a group of writers and educators who believed that writers could make a unique contribution to the teaching of writing. A non-profit organisation, T&W provides workshops for over 30,000 students per year. The Writer-in-Residence Programs help students, parents and teachers improve their writing skills and learn to write more imaginatively. T&W specialises in workshops in the following areas:

- poetry, fiction, playwriting and journalism;
- the literary and personal essay;
- memoir and journal writing;
- multicultural literature and writing;
- whole language learning;
- theatre improvisation for problem solving and conflict resolution;
- content-area writing (e.g. social studies, ecology, the sciences);
- children's literature;
- intergenerational writing projects.

T&W offers hands-on workshops for teachers and administrators all the subjects above. In 1992, T&W celebrated its 25th anniversary by opening the Center for Imaginative Writing, a resource library and meeting place for writers, educators, and students in the greater New York City area and a link to teachers and writers across the country.

T&W publishes an impressive catalogue of creative writing titles on very diverse topics, from The T&W Guide to Classic American Literature to The Adventures of Dr Alphabet. T&W books are now available in Britain via NAWE, and they are well worth exploring. The T&W website includes WriteNet: a valuable resource for writers and teachers interested in teaching imaginative writing. These pages feature articles by teachers and writers about fiction, poetry and teaching methods; online workshops and students' own poetry.

Writers In The Schools
Based in Houston, Texas, Writers In The Schools (WITS) has been sending professional poets, fiction writers, and playwrights into classrooms since 1983, to share their love and knowledge of the written word with students and teachers. WITS is also involved in national initiatives, such as mentoring other writers-in-schools programs, serving as a model for multidisciplinary arts educators, and designing curricula for use in schools.

The vision behind WITS is to revolutionise the way reading and writing are taught, nurturing the growth of the imagination and awakening students to the adventures of language. The programme is built on the principles that *"everyone has a personal story to tell"* and that *"every child deserves a holistic education that encourages critical thinking, creativity, and personal responsibility"*.

New Zealand
The New Zealand Book Council
Each year the New Zealand Book Council's Writers in Schools programme sends top Kiwi writers into schools to inspire and encourage young readers. Since 1972 the programme has provided free school visits for Book Council members, delivering excellence to a generation of New Zealand students, from the biggest city colleges to the tiniest country schools. Each year, over one hundred thousand students have a chance to meet their writing heroes at schools around the country. One teacher says, *"In a country where rugby players are the heroes, it is magnificent to have people from the book world to appear live in our school. What a boost for children that love to read, write and draw"*.

The Book Council offers member schools the opportunity to apply for one sponsored writer visit a year – visits are allocated on a first-come first-served basis. Current budgets allow over three hundred sponsored visits a year. In addition to this, the Book Council arranges additional visits if these are paid for by the school. As well as inspiring and motivating students, the scheme supports excellence in writing for children and adults by employing leading New Zealand authors. The New Zealand Book Council has published some useful guidelines on Hosting a Writer/Illustrator to Your School – these can be downloaded from the website and are equally relevant to writers-in-schools work here in Britain.

Breaking new ground

We have all inherited certain methodologies of working with young people. The 'writing in education' movement has grown organically over forty years from a few tiny seeds into a forest of activity. It has now reached a stage of maturity where we should take stock, learn from each other's experience and imagine new and more effective ways forward.

Whenever a writer is invited to work with students, an investment is made. This investment involves money, an especially precious resource in most schools. It involves time and energy on the part of hard-pressed teachers, writers and co-ordinators in the small organisations which make it happen. For this investment to pay the greatest dividends, we need to make an equal investment in imagination. Simply replicating the same structures and routines, project after project, without any element of reinvention, is not the best use of our collective resources. As one very experienced writer says, *"it's great if funders and programmers (arts councils, education authorities) and schools get briefed on the range of creative possibilities, so the work stays fresh and varied"*.

INNOVATION
Co-ordinators
There are some really adventurous projects going on, often led by small 'beacon' organisations, literature workers and project co-ordinators. They are well placed, a step back from the chalk-face, to observe the highs and lows, to notice and document what works well and what doesn't, to evaluate the success of projects and to spend time on research and 'blue-sky thinking'. They are exceptionally well networked, thanks to the National Association for Literature Development, which invests continually in their professional development and in research and advocacy.

Writers
It's all too easy for a writer to end up delivering the same workshop over and over again for twenty years. If it's a winning formula, why not? In a situation where most schools bookings are made on minimal forward planning, it can start to feel as though nothing more is required, or even possible. But this is a recipe for boredom and staleness, leading the writer to grow cynical about the schools work and start doing it on 'automatic pilot'.

If the infrastructure is strong and supportive, the writer is in a strong position to make bold alternative suggestions, to try things out and take a few risks, to *lead* the project rather than just implement it.

Teachers

Schools too should be innovators. Teachers are highly creative people and know their students well. Dreaming up a writing project is enjoyable, a chance to let your imagination off the leash. No teacher should ever be afraid to say "I've never done this before and I don't really know how to go about it". On the other hand, if they do have ideas, they should have the confidence to put them forward. Where there have been previous projects, consider alternatives rather than running a straightforward repeat which may not suit the new circumstances.

Start by thinking of what you would like to see happen in an ideal world: "Wouldn't it be great if we had a writer-in-residence for a whole year... just imagine what an impact that could have!" Allow yourself space to think the unthinkable; it can be scaled down or adapted afterwards, and by then you'll be fizzing with enthusiasm.

NEW DIRECTIONS

Here are a few suggestions for breaking new ground in your work with writers and schools:

Where?

Taking students out of school is a powerful action in itself. It allows new and alternative ways of working which would be difficult to achieve in the familiar environment and routines of the classroom. Anyone who has worked with a group of school children in a museum, an art gallery, a theatre or a shopping centre will remember how lively, engaged and excited they were. There are rich opportunities to make cross-curricular links with history, geography, art and science through the venue, its artefacts or the environment. Creative writing does not live in a space labelled 'English', and writers do not generate all their ideas from some internal factory called the imagination; being out in the world, having new and varied experiences, is vital.

It's important not to make too many assumptions, but to think openly and flexibly. The creative spark can come from surprising places: working in an art gallery, you may find that students write about the lifts, or about the cleaners polishing the floors, as well as about the paintings and sculptures.

"The writer had a lot of different resources and a classroom doesn't have much. We were actually able to look at the paintings instead of photocopies."
Year 6 pupil

Take the school to the writer

Novelists, poets, playwrights and storytellers give readings, have their work performed in theatres and hold book launches. Nothing will bring more energy to a project than for a group of pupils and teachers to come along and get a flavour of the writer's work in a different context. Think of it as the equivalent of the Geography field-trip! Reciprocal experiences like these demonstrate to young people that literature has a life beyond the page and beyond the English lesson; it's something spoken, performed and celebrated; something which attracts audiences and is valued and enjoyed in the wider world. GCSE Poetry Live! stages exciting performance events specifically for schools, and teachers should be on the lookout for other opportunities too. As a Sixth Form student says: *"It was brilliant to hear Simon Armitage read. There is something so special about hearing poems read by their author, it adds a whole new level to poetry – to actually see and listen to the person from whose head the words originally emerged"*.

What a shame we can't bring Wordsworth or Keats into the classroom! But we can take the pupils to 'meet' them by visiting their houses, which have been restored not only to look beautiful but also to offer real insight into their work. There are dozens of these 'lithouses' in Britain, and they would make wonderful venues for creative writing projects. Shandy Hall, the home of Laurence Sterne, now hosts a pioneering project called Asterisk, which aims to *"enable artists, technologists, academics and students to engage in narrative experiment and research"*; see more at www.asterisk.org.uk.

Different structures
A 30-day residency is an ambitious project. Feel free to experiment with different ways of scheduling the days. A dream for some busy writers is the residency which takes place over an extended period, such as ten days per term over the course of the whole year. Time between sessions allows pupils to reflect on their work, do some redrafting or make notes for future pieces.

On the other hand, the essential concept may be one of 'total immersion', an intense experience which touches every corner of the school. This calls for a great deal of advance planning. It will require a writer who can commit to full-time work for six weeks, and a staff with the enthusiasm, flexibility and team ethos to make it happen without feeling swamped.

More than one
Writing itself is essentially a solitary activity, but working in school need not always mirror this. A project can be specially designed to be led by a pair of writers, and justified to funders on that basis. Opportunities for joint planning must be built in to the budget. The two writers might be chosen for the closeness of their practice, or they might be from different genres or disciplines – what are the creative possibilities in pairing a novelist with a journalist, or a poet with a screenwriter? You want two writers who will spark off each other, reinforce each

101

other, offer the students two complementary approaches. A model for this way of working already exists: the Arvon Foundation's residential writing courses are jointly led by two writers, carefully chosen for compatibility and/or contrast (usually by asking one writer to nominate a partner). The advantages of this, in the words of the National Director Stephanie Anderson, are that *"not only does each student get more individual tutorial time... but having two writers with different writing backgrounds – and sometimes working in different genres – provides the emerging and developing writers with a broader and more useful experience"*.

Cross-artform
Consider the potential of a project which brings together a writer with a photographer, sculptor, dancer, musician or illustrator. It is vital to find the right artists who will get on and collaborate well, and to build in time for joint planning. Projects like this can be brilliantly successful in creating new and unusual work.

Writer swap
Breathe new life into two residencies – in different towns, regions or even countries – by exchanging writers for a day or two.

Involve parents
Involving parents is a very powerful way of adding value to a creative writing project. Parent volunteers might assist in a workshop, or asked to contribute at home to a collaborative piece of writing which draws in children, teachers, other school staff and local people. The writer may be interested in leading an after-school workshop specifically for parents. Samples of children's work can be sent home on the school letter, and parents can be invited to view an exhibition or attend a performance one evening in school. Make an occasion of it with a glass of wine and a chance to meet the writer.

Commission
Fellowships in Higher Education frequently include paid time for the writer to create new work. Why shouldn't this happen in a school setting too? Pupils will learn so much simply by watching the writer at work. Think about how the work can be valued and recognised through publication, performance, recording, public art, etc.

Virtual residency
The internet has opened up new opportunities for writers to interact with schools. At its simplest, the virtual project is an email exchange of writing exercises, drafts and feedback. It can also involve use of website technology to build collaborative writing between young people who have never met. The interactive whiteboard makes it possible for a writer and a whole class to meet and work

together 'live'. Videoconferencing offers the chance for young people in one country to encounter a writer on the other side of the world.

A few examples of projects to look at:

- www.pwynne.hostinguk.com/writing_together.htm *Young Voices from Birmingham*: Peter Wynne Wilson's residency for Writing Together.
- www.kotn.ntu.ac.uk Kids on the Net, run by the trAce Online Writing Centre, where you can read about Writers for the Future, a project exploring "innovative ways of writing using the internet".
- www.nesta.org.uk/ourawardees/profiles/4009 Adopt an Author, piloted by a group of literature festivals in 2004.
- A Writer in E-Residence: an account by Jack Todhunter of a project with novelist Steve Alton (Writing in Education 35, Spring 2005)

PUSHING THE BOUNDARIES
Schools and teachers have other concerns and priorities which writers can help address:

Writing for a range of purposes
Writers may not always be aware of the sheer volume and variety of writing tasks faced by pupils in the course of a school day. In English lessons alone, Key Stage 3 pupils are required to write for a range of purposes, only one of which is specifically designed around 'creative writing': *to imagine, explore and entertain.* The other three-quarters of the writing pupils do is *to inform, explain and describe; to persuade, argue and advise; and to analyse, review and comment.*

In most people's minds the 'creative' bit of creative writing is connected with story writing, drama or poetry – non-fiction is perceived as less exciting – but an author's visit can improve the quality of writing wherever it occurs. The line between fiction and non-fiction is one all writers cross routinely in their work. A novelist researches fact in order to create fiction; a poet might use autobiography as a starting point for fantasy.

Alan Gibbons, a teacher as well as a novelist, has Year 6 classes bubbling over with enthusiasm when he asks them to write a set of instructions; instead of deadly dull topics like 'how to heat soup in the microwave' or 'how to print a document', they write 'how to destroy a vampire'. His use of fiction to develop non-fiction writing makes it fun.

Recently moves have been made to broaden the range of visiting writers available to schools. Some organisations are beginning to work with writers of non-fiction, including journalism, travel writing and 'life writing' (biography, autobiography and memoir). It will take time to recruit and train writers in these fields, but they will surely be welcomed by many schools.

Cross-curricular

In subject areas other than English, teachers are increasingly open to the idea of bringing literature or creative writing into their teaching. In the context of the multiple priorities and enormous teaching load they have to manage, it's not surprising that only the most enthusiastic or well-supported History or Maths teachers go a stage further and invite a writer into the classroom. More often, projects of this kind are the initiative of an imaginative co-ordinator or organisation. They can involve a fair amount of advocacy, persuading the school to take the idea on board and making it work in a Science or Geography department where some staff remain to be convinced.

However, there is now a Literacy Co-ordinator in every school, whose job it is to ensure that reading and writing are valued and prioritised in all areas of the curriculum. They are often lateral thinkers who can bring a fresh approach to teaching and learning in any subject. Speaking of a project with writer Mario Petrucci linking science and creative writing, Judith Fouldes says: *"Now there's a requirement for literacy across the curriculum... as literacy co-ordinator as well as head of English, I could find that it is a burden. Other departments are not that focused on the literary aspects, as they are busy teaching their own subjects. So this day with a visiting writer is an attempt to kick-start a feeling for literacy across other subject areas"* (Times Educational Supplement).

Progression

English teachers often want to be able to identify how pupils make progress in creative writing – how their skills and attitudes develop over the course of the journey through school. Sue Horner, Head of English at the Qualifications and Curriculum Authority, issues a challenge to writers to examine the way they work with different age-groups: *"How should a visit by a writer be different if it is to 6 year olds or 13 year olds? Should we be content to find that activities and subjects which might be relevant to younger pupils are being repeated with older pupils? And it's not just topics, but techniques for writing. What more should be demanded of older pupils?"* (Writing in Education).

Assessment

Teachers are often concerned about how to tell whether a piece of writing is good, how to mark or grade it, and whether it is in fact possible to do so. Creative writing is often seen as occupying a special place beyond critical judgement, yet on the other hand we all make critical judgements about the books we read. Writers may be able to help teachers identify features which make a piece of writing exciting, effective or original, but they are unlikely to be able to solve the assessment issue. Sue Dymoke's book and Assessing Poetry (Sage, 2003) explores the subject with the thoroughness it requires.

WORKING WITH TRAINEE TEACHERS

In 2001, the Poetry Society teamed up with the School of Education at Exeter University to create a pioneering model for writers working with trainee teachers. The poet Ann Sansom worked with a group of students undergoing their Initial Teacher Training, and the classroom teachers they were paired with on their long teaching practice. It included intensive workshop days, and the planning and delivery of poetry projects in the classroom.

This pilot project was so overwhelmingly successful that it was repeated in 2003 with a different group and a different poet. One of the trainee teachers told us: "*I would never have had the confidence to teach poetry had I not taken part in this, but now I can't wait to teach it again!*". Teachers in the area continue to talk about the impact it has had on their professional lives.

The Exeter project was made possible by two things: the extraordinary enthusiasm and imagination of staff in the university department, and money from the poetryclass project (funded at that time by the DfES). We are aware of several other instances of work in this area, led by keen individuals (notably at London Metropolitan University and Bath Spa University College). Writing workshops usually take place as an 'extra', in the students' own time, and are made possible by goodwill and minimal funding. But if we are serious about raising standards in writing and promoting creativity in schools, *all* trainee teachers should have the opportunity to learn about creative writing from a real writer. The costs are relatively low, and the investment pays huge dividends. Those Exeter teachers are now in post in schools all over Britain, where they are able to share what they learnt with colleagues and continue making a real difference to the young people they teach.

TOWARDS PROFESSIONALISM

Many of our recommendations to writers are about becoming more professional in the way we approach schools work. This doesn't mean losing any of our creative spark, or compromising the originality of what we bring to the classroom; far from it. It means adding strength and flexibility, not taking anything away.

Organisation

Many of us may resent the stereotype of the disorganised writer, but comments from project organisers suggest that problems do persist. Professionalism means taking all our responsibilities seriously, including irritating details such as turning up to meetings, getting to school on time, making phone calls, getting photocopying done in advance, etc, etc.

Investment in ourselves

As freelancers it is up to us to get the balance right: to continue to invest in our careers as writers, to accept or decline offers of work according to our own priorities and to make sure we get the training and professional development we need.

Confidence

If we want schools to trust us to deliver exciting and worthwhile projects, we need to have the confidence to take control. We are not instruments of any curriculum or policy but professional writers with our own ideas and methods. We need to listen too, but we should trust ourselves and our own expertise. We know what we're talking about!

GLOSSARY

ADHD	Attention Deficit it Hyperactivity Disorder
AVA	Audio Visual Aids (overhead projector, TV, video, etc)
EBD	Emotional and Behavioral Difficulties
DfES	Department for Education & Skills
EAZ	Education Action Zones
EiC	Excellence in Cities
ESTYN	Her Majesty's Inspectorate for Education and Training in Wales
G & T	Gifted & Talented
Hard outcomes	Measurable results of a project, such as improved literacy skills
HMIS	Her Majesty's Inspector of Schools, Scotland
HLTA	Higher Level Teaching Assistant
ICT	Information and Communications Technology
INSET	In-Service Training for teachers
Key Stages	The National Curriculum in England and Wales has five Key Stages setting out what pupils must study at school and when (see the Standards Site for details)
Soft outcomes	Results of a project which are not easily quantifiable, such as enjoyment or improved confidence
LEA	Local Education Authority (run by each local council and responsible for all aspects of education)
League Tables	Information about individual schools in England and Wales, based on SATs results and published
MLD	Moderate Learning Difficulties
OFSTED	Office for Standards in Education (school inspectorate in England)
Partner Schools	Primary schools that, because of their locality, provide the new intake of pupils to a secondary school at the start of the school year (previously known as Feeder Schools)
PMLD	Profound and Multiple Learning Difficulties
Primary School	Schools for children aged from 4 - 11
PTA	Parent Teacher Association
SATs	Standard Assessment Tests, taken at ages 7, 11 and 14 (England and Wales only)
Secondary school	Schools for young people aged from 11 to 18
SED	Scottish Education Department
SEN	Special Educational Needs
SENCo	Special Educational Needs Co-ordinator
SLD	Severe Learning Difficulties
Special Measures	Imposed on schools judged by Inspectors to have low attainment and poor progress
SPTEC	Scottish Parent Teacher Council
QCA	Qualifications and Curriculum Authority

BIBLIOGRAPHY

A & C Black: *Writers' & Artists' Yearbook 2005*

Arts Council England, 2003: *From Looking Glass to Spyglass*

Arts Victoria, 2002: *Evaluating Community Arts and Community Well Being*

Barrs, M and Rosen, M (ed): *A Year with Poetry*
CLPE, 1997

Collins, B: *Filling Tennyson's Shoes: A Tête-à-Tête with the Laureates*
Teachers & Writers, vol 35 no 3

Cookson, P: *The very best of Paul Cookson*
www.poetryzone.co.uk

Croft, A: *Excluded*
www.poetryclass.net

Dymoke, S: *Assessing your pupils' poetry*
 www.poetryclass.net

Dymoke, S: *Drafting and Assessing Poetry: A Guide for Teachers*
Paul Chapman, 2003

Fincham, L: *Roget's Thesaurus Puts It Neatly*
Writing in Education, Issue 22

Garner, A: *The Voice that Thunders*
Harvill, 1998

Goodwin, M and Tyler-Bennett, D (ed): *Poetry, Prose and Playfulness for Teachers and Learners*
Leicestershire County Council, 2004

Hooper, K: *Root and Branch*
Times Educational Supplement, 1 October 2004

Hughes, T: *Poetry in the Making: An Anthology of Poems and Programmes from "Listening and Writing"*
Faber & Faber, 1986

Kearney, R: *On Stories*
Taylor & Francis Books, 2001

Marzan, J (ed): *Luna, Luna: Creative Writing ideas from Spanish, Latin American and Latino Literature*
Teachers and Writers Collaborative, 2000

McGregor, S: *Squaring the literary circle*
Times Educational Supplement (Scotland), 18 March 2005

Morley, D and Mortimer, A (ed): *Under the Rainbow: Writers & Artists in Schools*
Bloodaxe, 1991

Mort, G: *The Poetryclass Interview*
www.poetryclass.net

Moses, B: *Inviting a poet into your school*
www.poetryzone.ndirect.co.uk

Munden, P: *Mavericks and the Curriculum*
Teachers & Writers, vol 35 no 3

Neumark, V: *Escape to the Witty Planet*
Times Educational Supplement, 1 October 2004

Orfali, A: *Artists working in partnership with schools*
Arts Council England, 2004

Peters, A F: *Simile, metaphor, conceit and personification*
The Poetry Book for Primary Schools, Poetry Society, 1999
Pratchett, T: interviewed by Adam Binding and Hannah Giannini
Young Writer magazine, April 1996
Pullman, P: *Theatre – the true key stage*
The Guardian, 30 March 2004
Robinson, Professor K: *Creating Room for Creativity*
Times Educational Supplement, 21 May 1999
Rosen, M: *Did I Hear You Write?*
Five Leaves, 1989
S'ari, S: *Blueprint for Success*
Times Educational Supplement, 1 October 2004
Scottish Arts Council/Children in Scotland, 2004: *Creating Safety: child protection guidelines for the arts*
Scottish Book Trust, 2004: *Literature Alive! Working with Writers, a guideline and resource*
Shapiro, N L and Padgett, R (ed): *The Point: Where Teaching and Writing Intersect*
Teachers & Writers Collaborative, 1983
South Bank Centre, 2004: *A Special Place: Poems by members of Gwynedd Writing Squads*
Sprackland, J (ed): *National Poetry Day booklet for schools*
Poetry Society, 2002 (*Celebration*) and 2004 (*Food*)
Styles, M and Cook, H (ed): *There's a poet behind you*
A & C Black, 1988
Sweeney, M and Williams, J H: *Writing Poetry and getting published*
Hodder & Stoughton, 1997
Turner, B (ed): *The Writer's Handbook*
Macmillan, 2005
Wilson, A: *Better than double English: how useful are poets in schools?*
 Writing in Education, Spring 1998
Wilson, A and Hughes, S: *The Poetry Book for Primary Schools*
Poetry Society, 1998
Wilson, J: interviewed by Ruth Bircham and pupils from the Dunway School
Young Writer magazine, April 2000
Yates, C: *Jumpstart: Poetry in the Secondary School*
Poetry Society, 1999
Wright, K: interviewed by pupils from King's School, Plymouth
Young Writer magazine, January 2000
Zielgler, A: *The Writing Workshop Vol 1*
Teachers & Writers Collaborative, 1981

FURTHER READING

Boran, P: *The Portable Creative Writing Workshop*
Salmon Publishing, 1999
Brownjohn, S: *Does it Have to Rhyme?*
Hodder & Stoughton, 1980
Corbett, P and Moses, B: *Catapults and Kingfishers: Teaching Poetry in Primary Schools*

Oxford University Press, 1986
Koch, K: *Rose Where Did You Get That Red? Teaching Great Poetry to Children*
Random House, 1973
Koch, K: *Wishes, Lies and Dreams: Teaching Children to Write Poetry*
Harper Collins, 1970
Sansom, P: *Writing Poems*
Bloodaxe Books, 1994
The School Library Association: *Brilliant Books: Running a Successful School Library Book Event*, 2005
Willis, M S: *Deep revision: a guide for teachers, students and other writers*
Teachers and Writers Collaborative, 1993

PARTNERS

The following organisations supported the writing and publication of this book:

The National Association for Literature Development (NALD) is the professional body for all those involved in the development of creative writing and reading. The organisation exists so that literature professionals can talk to each other through the newsletter, website and events. NALD values and passes on skills and knowledge through its professional development programme, and makes the case for increased investment in literature development. It provides Professional Development opportunities for literature specialists, including day seminars, a residential and ongoing mentoring and seminar programmes for new and experienced literature activists.
NALD, PO Box 140, Ilkley LS29 7WP
01943 862107
www.nald.org

The National Association of Writers in Education (NAWE) is a membership organisation, supporting the work of writers and teachers in developing creative writing in all educational settings throughout the UK. NAWE aims to ensure that writers are really well prepared for the work that they do in schools, and that teachers can make the most of them. NAWE leads the *literaturetraining* programme, providing full support for the professional development of writers and others working in the literature sector.

Conferences, which are open to anyone, bring writers (and teachers) together in order to share their practice and learn from others' workshop ideas. The magazine, *Writing in Education*, features articles and reports of writing workshops and larger projects in schools and other educational contexts. All of these resources are also accessible via the NAWE website, though some areas are restricted to members.

NAWE also maintains the *artscape* website, a national directory of writers and other artists who work in schools and community settings. All those listed in this directory are experienced at working in education and have Enhanced Disclosures from the CRB. References are published as part of each individual's record. NAWE membership is £20 per annum and brings you the magazine three times per year, regular newsletters and reduced rate booking for all conferences, training days, mentoring schemes and other events. NAWE has the facilities to process Disclosure checks and can guide individuals through this procedure.

NAWE, PO Box 1, Sheriff Hutton, York YO60 7YU
01653 618429
info@nawe.co.uk
www.nawe.co.uk
www.artscape.org.uk (directory of writers)

The Poetry Society is one of Britain's most high profile arts organisations and has over 3,000 members around the world. If you read, write or enjoy poetry, the Poetry Society can open up the world of contemporary poetry for you.

The Poetry Society has an outstanding reputation for its exciting and innovative education work. For nearly thirty years it has been introducing poets into classrooms, providing comprehensive teachers' resources and producing colourful, accessible publications for pupils. Amongst its many education resources are the Poets in Schools scheme, over thirty years of introducing poets into classrooms; and poetryclass, a unique training programme for teachers. In recent years the Poetry Society has worked with Education Action Zones, Excellence in Cities clusters and LEAs to develop larger-scale projects. The Poetry Society also runs the Foyle Young Poets of the Year Award, the premier youth poetry competition for 11- 17 year olds.
The Poetry Society, 22 Betterton Street, London WC2H 9BX
020 7420 9880
education@poetrysociety.org.uk
www.poetrysociety.org.
www.poetryclass.net (online poetry classroom)

Writing Together is a unique partnership of book and literature charities and official bodies. Booktrust hosts the project, and The Poetry Society and the National Association of Writers in Education work with QCA, the national strategies, Arts Council England and the DfES. Andrew Motion, poet laureate, is a major figure, and there are a number of patrons including Simon Armitage, UA Fanthorpe, Richard Eyre, Julie Myerson, Jackie Kay, Michael Boyd, Simon Schama, David Almond, Fiona Shaw, Fred D'Aguiar, David Edgar, Blake Morrison and Louis de Bernieres.

Writing Together aims to ensure that, during their life at school, every child encounters opportunities to work with professional writers who inspire them to write creatively.

The ideas Writing Together has been developing are relevant and significant for teachers of all ages of pupils, and have the potential for encouraging creativity and inspiring young writers. This increases pupils' commitment to and achievement in writing, and also promotes their reading. Teachers who have planned, carried out and evaluated writers' work in schools are convinced that it has positive effects for pupils and for the school as a whole.
Writing Together, Booktrust, 45 East Hill, London SW18 2QZ
0208 516 2976
writingtogether@booktrust.org.uk

USEFUL ORGANISATIONS

Arts Council England
14 Great Peter Street, London SW1P 3NQ
0845 300 6200
www.artscouncil.org.uk

The Arts Council/An Chomhairle Ealaìon
70 Merrion Square, Dublin 2, Republic of Ireland
00 353 1 618 0200
www.artscouncil.ie

The Arts Council of Northern Ireland
MacNeice House, 77 Malone Road, Belfast BT9 6AQ
www.artscouncil-ni.org

Scottish Arts Council
12 Manor Place, Edinburgh EH3 7DD
www.scottisharts.org.uk

The Arts Council of Wales
Museum Place, Cardiff CF10 3NX
www.artswales.org.uk/language

Academi is the Welsh National Literature Promotion Agency and Society of Writers. Academi runs events, courses, competitions, conferences, tours by authors and international exchanges. Its literature funding schemes assist writers visits to schools, libraries, prisons, writers groups, festivals, women's institutes, marched y wawr branches, out-of-school hours groups, environmental groups, arts centres and any organisation using creative writers to deliver literature workshops, lectures and readings. Year-on-year the Academi funds around 1,400 events reaching 100,000 people of all ages.
3rd floor, Mount Stuart House, Mount Stuart Square, Cardiff CF10 5FQ
029 2047 2266
post@academi.org
www.academi.org

Apples & Snakes is England's leading organiser of performance poetry, established in 1982 as a platform for poetry which would be popular, relevant, cross-cultural and accessible to the widest possible range of people. Apples & Snakes has education at the core of its mission and carries out a wide range of educational activities, of which the extremely successful Poets in Education Scheme is an integral part.
BAC, Lavender Hill SW11 5TN
020 7738 0941
lisa@applesandsnakes.org
www.applesandsnakes.org

The Arvon Foundation's aims are to provide residential courses that ignite a love of imaginative writing and develop the creative voice of each participant. As one teacher described it, 'the residential was an assured recipe for creative empowerment'. Each course is individually created for each group and Arvon can match professional writers to the wishes and requirements of each particular group in any writing genres and across all forms. The courses are subsidised by Arvon in line with our open access policy. Full funding is possible in certain circumstances. Arvon also runs a grant scheme to enable teachers to attend adult courses.

Arvon, The Foundation for Writing, 42a Buckingham Palace Road, London SW1W 0RE
020 7931 7611
b.lyon@arvonfoundation.org
www.arvonfoundation.org

Book Communications is an independent partnership which undertakes project management, training, research, marketing and fundraising for the arts sector, focusing on creative writing and reading.
Unit 116, The Custard Factory, Gibb Street, Birmingham, B9 4AA
0121 246 2770
jonathan.davidson@dial.pipex.com

Booktrust is the national organisation bringing books and people together from the start. They run book prizes and brilliant projects to encourage readers of all ages and cultures to discover and enjoy books and reading. These include: Bookstart, the national books for babies scheme; Children's Book Week, the annual celebration of reading for pleasure; The Children's Laureate, The Booktrust Teenage Prize, John Llewellyn Rhys Prize, Bookscapes, Writing Together and other innovative work with writers and readers.
45 East Hill, London SW18 2QZ
020 8516 2977
info@booktrust.org.uk
www.booktrust.org.uk
www.booktrusted.com *(the website for teachers, parents and all those who care what young people read)*

The British Council Literature Department promotes innovative and contemporary work from the UK, and builds audiences for international literature through its global network. It works with hundreds of artists all over the world, leads over 350 projects, hosts many websites and publishes widely.
10 Spring Gardens, London SW1A 2BN
020 7389 3194
Norwich Union House, 7 Fountain Street, Belfast BT1 5EG
028 9024 8220
The Tun, 3rd Floor, 4 Jackson's Entry, Holyrood Road, Edinburgh EH8 8PJ
0131 524 5714
28 Park Place, Cardiff CF10 3QE
029 20 397 346
www.britishcouncil.org

Children's Discovery Centre has been working with schools and writers for over twenty years to engage children in the pleasure and power of reading and writing. It now works with over 15,000 children every year, organising residencies, workshops and events in schools across England. Originally set up by teachers, the Children's Discovery Centre makes it easy for a school to work with a writer. Using only the best and most reliable authors, it takes care of all the administrative aspects of the visits.

Trident Centre, Bickersteth Road, Tooting Broadway, London SW17 9SH
020 8767 4551
info@childrensdiscovery.org.uk
www.childrensdiscovery.org.uk

Commonword /Cultureword is a creative writing and publishing organisation that serves new writers and readers from all kinds of communities in the North West. It provides the facilities for people to develop their writing, and its activities act as a point of focus for many writers seeking encouragement and confidence. Commonword and Cultureword co-ordinate a range of Writing Development and Publishing Projects, often in collaboration with other organisations, including schools.
6 Mount Street, Manchester M2 5NS
0161 832 3777
enquiries@commonword.org.uk
www.commonword.org.uk

Creative Partnerships provides school children across England with the opportunity to develop creativity in learning and to take part in cultural activities of the highest quality. It is not a funding body but aims to establish genuine collaborative partnerships to enable the development of projects that reflect the interests, specialisms and shared vision of those involved.
Arts Council England, 14 Great Peter Street, London SW1P 3NQ
0845 300 6200
info@creative-partnerships.com
www.creative-partnerships.com

Derby Literature Development is based within the arts team at the City Council, Derby Literature Development supports and co-ordinates a range of activity for readers and writers in Derby, including advice on funding, creative opportunities, writers in schools and live events. It co-ordinates Derby's Festival of Words, a celebration of literature in the city, featuring live performance, stories, poetry, food, films and books. It also produces two publications: Word of Mouth (a quarterly magazine) and Live Words in Derby (an email bulletin with information about opportunities for writers).
Derby City Council, Roman House, Friar Gate, Derby DE1 1XB
01332 715434
naomi.wilds@derby.gov.uk
www.derbysfestivalofwords.co.uk

The Federation of Worker Writers and Community Publishers is a non-profit making umbrella organisation for writers' groups and community publishers. Membership is open to all organisations working with words and language who share a belief that writing and publishing should be made accessible to all. Formed in 1976, FWWCP now has member groups and organisations in the UK and around the World.
Burslem School of Art, Queen Street, Stoke-on-Trent, Staffs ST6 3EJ
01782 822327
fwwcp@tiscali.co.uk
http://thefwwcp.org.uk

Lapidus is a membership organisation, established in 1996 to promote the use of the literary arts - that is: reading, writing and performing of poetry, prose, fiction or drama; storytelling; journal writing - for personal development. Its members include writers and poets, librarians, medical and healthcare professionals, therapists and service users, academics, teachers and those having a general interest in the field.
BM Lapidus, London WC1N 3XX
info@lapidus.org.uk
www.lapidus.org.uk

Literaturetraining provides information and advice on professional development for writers and others involved in creating or supporting new writing and literature. Its online directory at www.literaturetraining.com acts as a first stop shop for up-to-the-minute information on training and professional development opportunities in the UK. Other services include a fortnightly e-bulletin service, a developing range of resource materials on key topics relating to creative and professional practice, a free information and advice service, and professional development planning guidance.
PO Box 23595, Leith EH6 7YX
0131 553 2210
philippa@literaturetraining.com
www.literaturetraining.com

Live Literature Scotland (based at Scottish Book Trust) is a unique funding scheme which takes Scottish writers to every corner of Scottish society. They have an online database of writers, Words@Work, a professional development programme for writers and they support up to 1500 events a year in schools, libraries, hospitals and communities throughout Scotland. Live Literature Schools is a new initiative focusing on work in schools (contact Louise Anderson on 0131 524 0166 for more information). See Scottish Book Trust for contact details.

The National Literacy Trust, founded in 1993, is an independent charity dedicated to building a literate nation. It provides a web-based literacy support network which pulls together the best ideas and information to help everyone share good practice; and leads practical initiatives such as Reading Is Fundamental, the National Reading Campaign and Talk To Your Baby.
Swire House, 59 Buckingham Gate, London SW1E 6AJ
020 7828 2435
contact@literacytrust.org.uk
www.literacytrust.org.uk

New Writing North is the writing development agency for the north east of England. It aims to create an environment in the north east of England in which new writing in all genres can flourish and develop. NWN is a unique organisation within the UK, merging individual development work with writers across all media with educational work and the production of creative projects.
2 School Lane, Whickham NE16 4SL
0191 488 8580
mail@newwritingnorth.com
www.newwritingnorth.com

The Poetry Book Society The PBS is a specialist poetry bookseller and a book club for everyone who enjoys poetry - dedicated readers, occasional browsers and absolute beginners. The PBS aims to foster a love of contemporary poetry in a wide range of readers - including those in the classroom. There are two special membership schemes for teachers, children and teenagers, providing the usual package of information and discounts on the best newly published books, together with poetry posters, teaching tips and poetry discussion ideas. Call or email for a free information pack (please specify primary or secondary).
Book House, 45 East Hill, London SW18 2QZ
020 8870 8403
info@poetrybooks.co.uk
www.poetrybooks.co.uk

Poetry Can is a poetry development agency working throughout Bristol, South Gloucestershire, and Bath and NE Somerset. It provides information, advice and support on all aspects of poetry; it organises a lifelong learning programme of work including work with schools; it organises live poetry events including the annual Bristol Poetry Festival. Poetry Can is a registered charity.
Unit 11, Kuumba Project, Hepburn Road, Bristol BS2 8UD
0117 942 6976
info@poetrycan.demon.co.uk
www.poetrycan.co.uk

Poetry Ireland/Éigse Éireann is the national organisation for poetry in Ireland. It serves all 32 counties and receives support from The Arts Council of Ireland/An Chomhairle Ealaíon and The Arts Council of Northern Ireland. Its remit is to act as a resource and information point for everything to do with poetry in Ireland, serving poets, writers, academics and any member of the public with an interest in poetry.
120 St. Stephen's Green, Dublin 2
0353 1 478 9974
poetry@iol.ie
www.poetryireland.ie

The Poetry Library is the major library for modern and contemporary poetry, housing the most comprehensive and accessible collection of poetry from 1912 in Britain. Poetry is available in many formats: from books to magazines to posters and postcards for reference. There are comprehensive education and children's sections. The Poetry Library promotes the reading of poetry for people of all ages, cultures and backgrounds through its education programme and events. The Poetry Library will be closed for visits from the public during the Royal Festival Hall refurbishment (April 2005 – January 2007). The enquiry service will continue as normal.
Level 5, Royal Festival Hall, South Bank Centre, London
020 7921 0943
www.poetrylibrary.org.uk

The Poetry Trust The flagship literature organisation for the East of England, funded by Arts Council England. The Trust promotes high quality contemporary poetry and works to increase people's enjoyment of reading, writing and teaching poetry. Its 2-year creative

116

education project, Poetry Matters (funded by The Paul Hamlyn Foundation) offers writing workshops for teachers and students, residencies and live poetry performances in schools. The Trust organises the renowned international Aldeburgh Poetry Festival, held annually over the first weekend in November; the Jerwood Aldeburgh First Collection Prize; a Young Poets Competition and a wide range of courses and events.
The Cut, 9 New Cut, Halesworth, Suffolk IP19 8BY
01986 835950
info@thepoetrytrust.org
www.thepoetrytrust.org

The School Library Association The SLA believes that every pupil is entitled to effective school library provision. The SLA is committed to supporting everyone involved with school libraries, promoting high quality reading and learning opportunities for all.
Unit 2, Lotmead Business Village, Lotmead Farm, Wanborough, Swindon SN4 0UY
01793 791787
info@SLA.org.uk
www.sla.org.uk

Scottish Book Trust is Scotland's national agency for reading and writing, a unique organisation committed to the promotion of reading and books. Scottish Book Trust believes in the value of making every child a reading child, every adult a reading adult, and every reader a lover of good books.
Sandeman House, Trunk's Close, 55 High Street, Edinburgh
EH1 1SR
0131 524 0160
info@scottishbooktrust.com
www.scottishbooktrust.com

The Scottish Poetry Library is the place for poetry in Scotland, for the regular reader, the serious student or the casual browser. Since its foundation in 1984 it has amassed a remarkable collection of written works, as well as tapes and videos. The emphasis is on contemporary poetry written in Scotland, in Scots, Gaelic and English, but historic Scottish poetry and contemporary works from almost every part of the world feature too. All resources, advice and information are readily accessible, free of charge.
5 Crichton's Close, Canongate, Edinburgh EH8 8DT
0131 557 2876
inquiries@spl.org.uk
www.spl.org.uk

The Society of Authors is a non-profit making organisation, founded in 1884, "to protect the rights and further the interests of authors". Today it has more than 7,500 members writing in all areas of the profession.
84 Drayton Gardens, London SW10 9SB
020 7373 6642
www.societyofauthors.net

The Scottish Storytelling Centre The Scottish Storytelling Forum is Scotland's national charity for storytelling. It was founded in 1992 to encourage and support the telling and sharing of stories across all ages and all sectors of society in particular those who, for

reasons of poverty or disability, were excluded from artistic experiences. The Scottish Storytelling Centre supports the national network, organising regular storytelling events, training workshops, and coordinating projects at local, national and international level.
43-45 High Street, Edinburgh EH1 1SR
0131 557 5724 / 556 9579
scottishstorytellingcentre@uk.uumail.com
www.scottishstorytellingcentre.co.uk

The Society for Storytelling is an open organisation which welcomes anyone with an interest in oral storytelling, whether teller, listener, beginner or professional. There are subgroups to cater for specialist interests such as storytelling in Education or Therapy. Since June 1993 they have been active in bringing like minded people together to enjoy, discuss and practice the art of storytelling.
P.O. Box 2344, Reading RG6 7FG
0118 935 1381
SfS@fairbruk.demon.co.uk
www.sfs.org.uk

Spread the Word supports the development of new writing and live literature in London. It has placed a range of novelists and poets in schools, arts centres, colleges and libraries. They have been chosen for their experience in workshop facilitation and the particular skills and know-how they bring to the project. Often they have specialised in a particular area of creative writing and the arts, such as writing for the stage, poetry or short fiction. Events and activities have ranged from a one-off reading and talk event to a week-long residency in a school.
77 Lambeth Walk, London SE11 6DX
020 7735 3111
info@spreadtheword.org.uk
www.spreadtheword.org.uk

The Reading Agency came into being in July 2002 as a UK wide development agency with its roots in the public library sector. It is founded on the principle that reading has infinite potential for making life richer and that libraries are the most democratic medium for bringing reading to people.
PO Box 96, St. Albans AL1 3WP
info@readingagency.org.uk
www.readingagency.org.uk

trAce connects writers and readers around the world in real and virtual space. It promotes an accessible and inclusive approach to the internet with the focus on creativity, collaboration and training. trAce also manages Kids on the Net, a site for young people featuring writing by children at home and at school all over the world. trAce encourages submissions of poems, stories, and contributions to its Friends, Opinions and All About Me pages. It also works with libraries, communities, teachers and schools on- and off-line to create web-specific writing projects.
The Nottingham Trent University, Clifton Lane, Nottingham NG11 8NS
0115 8486360
trace@ntu.ac.uk
http://trace.ntu.ac.uk

Ty Newydd / Taliesin Trust Ty Newydd is the National Writers' Centre for Wales. Residential courses are held on all aspects of creative writing in both English and Welsh. These include courses specifically for schools. Courses usually run from Monday to Saturday, but shorter courses can be arranged. Writers who have tutored courses in the past include Gillian Clarke, Jan Mark, Jackie Kay, Robert Minhinnick, Ian McMillan and Alan Plater. Ty Newydd can accommodate 16 pupils and two teachers and is located in beautiful countryside on the North Wales coast.
Ty Newydd, Llanystumdwy, Cricieth, Gwynedd LL52 0LW
01766 522 811
post@tynewydd.org
www.tynewydd.org

The Verbal Arts Centre is an educational charity promoting language arts, celebration of commonality and diversity, development of knowledge, understanding and excellence in creation, performance and critical practice across the verbal arts forms, together with research, publication and provision of information.
Stable Lane and Mall Wall, Bishop Street Within Derry/ Londonderry BT48 6PU
www.verbalartscentre.co.uk

The Windows Project is an independent educational charity, founded in 1976. Windows works in partnership with schools, libraries, hospitals, care centres, community organisations, play schemes and youth centres, running creative writing, performance and publishing projects for all ages and abilities. Windows works with professional writers including performance poets, storytellers, playwrights and children's novelists. All of them are experienced workshop leaders, educators and communicators of their craft.
Liver House, 96 Bold Street, Liverpool L1 4HY
0151 709 3688
windows@windowsproject.demon.co.uk
www.windowsproject.demon.co.uk

The Word Hoard is a co-operative of artists, whose members are writers, visual artists, performers and musicians, based in Huddersfield, West Yorkshire, England. It works with text, music, performance, film and the visual arts, in a variety of contexts with a huge range of people. The Word Hoard also brings artists from abroad to the UK, to play a part in its projects and to work and teach around the country.
Unit 25, The Gatehouse Centre, Albert Street, Huddersfield HD1 3QD
West Yorkshire
01484 426 626
hoard@zoo.co.uk
www.wordhoard.co.uk

Write On aims to promote the long-term benefits of all forms of writing in schools. Pupils and staff from over sixty schools per year across the West Midlands have been working with professional writers (from novelists to journalists) to inspire their own writing.
Birmingham Book Festival, c/o Unit 116, The Custard Factory, Gibb Street, Birmingham B9 4AA
0121 2462770
jonathan@bookcommunications.co.uk
www2.bgfl.org/writeontoo

writernet provides writers for all forms of live and recorded performance - working at any stage in their career, and in diverse contexts - with a range of services which enable them to pursue their careers.
Cabin V, Clarendon Buildings, 25 Horsell Road, London N5 1XL
020 7609 7474
info@writernet.org.uk
www.writernet.org.uk

The Writers' Guild of Great Britain represents writers in TV, film, radio, theatre, animation and books. Members benefit from access to specialist advice and information, legal services, regular events and publications.
15, Britannia Street, London WC1X 9JN
020 7833 0777
admin@writersguild.org.uk
http://cgi.writersguild.force9.co.uk

WEBSITES

Barrington Stoke is an award-winning publisher that specialises exclusively in fiction and resources for reluctant, dyslexic, disenchanted and under-confident readers and their teachers. The website includes useful resources for teachers, parents and pupils.
www.barringtonstoke.co.uk

This **BBC** web site provides online interactive literacy activities for early childhood and primary school students including resources for teachers in Northern Ireland.
www.bbc.co.uk/schools/4_11/literacy.shtml

The Centre for Studies on Inclusive Education is an excellent resource. An independent centre, it works in the UK and overseas to promote inclusion and end segregation. It is funded by donations from trusts, foundations and grants.
http://inclusion.uwe.ac.uk

Cherrybite Publications Competition Bulletin (bi-monthly) includes information on which competitions are open to young people.
www.cherrybite.co.uk

Children's Laureate Website
childrenslaureate.org

Click Thinking is about personal safety on the internet, providing downloadable advice and guidance.
www.scotland.gov.uk/clickthinking

The Count Me In Calendar is funded by Whitbread and is an invaluable tool for citizenship co-ordinators, school assembly planners and librarians: a comprehensive, free listing of charity awareness and fundraising campaigns.
www.countmeincalendar.info

Evaluation
www.evaluationforall.org.uk

International Association of School Librarians (IASL)
www.iasl-slo.org/

Kids Own Publishing aims to raise the status of children's creative skills as writers and artists by publishing materials written and illustrated by children.
www.kidsown.ie

Learning and Teaching Scotland
www.ltscotland.org.uk

Learning Wales is the Welsh Assembly's education website.
www.learning.wales.gov.uk

Literature North East is a one-stop-shop for what's happening in the world of literature in the North East of England.
www.literaturenortheast.co.uk

The London Schools Arts Service site provides an up-to-date online database of insured, CRB-checked artists and arts organisations from all arts sectors available to work in London schools. Other items include step by step guidance on setting up arts projects and forming arts partnerships, guidance on applying for funding, information on arts awards and initiatives, resources, borough contacts, case studies, news and events.
www.lonsas.org.uk

The National Grid for Learning is 'the gateway to educational resources on the internet'. It includes a wealth of information specific to Northern Ireland, Scotland and Wales as well as England.
www.ngfl.gov.uk

Poetry Kit features information on contemporary British poetry and poets.
www.poetrykit.org

Poetry Zone is a site containing children's poems, articles and teaching resources.
www.poetryzone.co.uk

The Society for Children's Book Writers & Illustrators is an international organisation for writers and illustrators of children's books. There is a range of resources on the website, including author profiles.
www.wordpool.co.uk

The Standards Site is the website of the Department for Education and Skills.
www.standards.dfes.gov.uk

Young Writer magazine is published three times a year (also available on cassette).
www.mystworld.com/youngwriter

Young Cultural Creators aims to encourage librarians, teachers, and educators in museums, archives and galleries all over the world, to set up their own YCC programmes and to share their experiences and good practice in a world-wide network.
www.youngculturalcreators.com

Youth Arts Online is a portal for young people who want information about opportunities in the arts, for youth arts practitioners and organisations.
www.youthartsonline.org/youthartson

INDEX